SHOW US THE

FATHER

—— 7 Secrets ——

TO BE A FATHER ON EARTH LIKE THE FATHER IN HEAVEN

SHOW US THE
FATHER

— 7 SECRETS —

TO BE A FATHER ON EARTH LIKE THE FATHER IN HEAVEN

Totus Tuus
— PRESS —

DEVIN SCHADT

Published by Totus Tuus Press
PO Box 280021
Lakewood, CO 80228

Cover design by Devin Schadt
Typesetting by Loyola Dataworks
Printed in the United States of America

ISBN 978-1-944578-91-6 (hardcover)
ISBN 978-1-944578-90-9 (paperback)
Library of Congress Control Number: 2015959693

CONTENTS

INTRODUCTION

Imagine that you and your family are dwelling in a war-torn land, amidst continual gunfire, the sporadic explosion of bombs, and military violence. Your wife and children are constantly in harm's way. Your neighborhood is a battleground and is overshadowed by the looming darkness of impending death and the threat of starvation, while you as the father are frantically attempting to find ways to protect and feed your family. Yet on the horizon, within the scope of human vision, exists the "glorious city," whose light never fades, where peace always reigns and lush fruit is always on the vine. You have one goal: to get your family there—alive.

There is, however, one obstacle: between you and the celestial city is an impassable, bramble-infested, thorn-thicketed forest. The deadly forest's breadth is too wide and too high to circumvent. The only way to the glorious city is to cut a path directly through the forest.

After making the decision to escape, you and your family flee and finally arrive at the outer edge of the immense sea of bramble, and you—knowing that your family must cut through this forest—turn to your wife and graciously voice those virtuous, noble, and heroic words that every woman desires to hear: "Honey, you go first."

It's not exactly the ideal script for an Academy Award-winning motion picture—because it wouldn't win any awards. The story would never sell because no one would want to buy it. We long for more. You and I, we fathers, are called to cut a path though the thicket of this world, this vale of tears, with the purpose of leading our families to the Fatherland where there exists bliss, ecstasy, joy, and eternal peace. We long to be the hero, but in order to do so, we must set the pace of self-giving love.

The man who believes that his identity exists in adventure, battles, and beauties may be on to something. However, these things merely hint at a deeper, more profound masculine essence—man's true identity. True manhood isn't achieved by wandering in the wilderness, conquering kingdoms, and winning the woman. The battle is not so much outside of us as it is inside each of us. We don't have to go out in search of it. No, the battle has found us; it is on the doorstep of our souls.

God has already established the battleground, the path, and the adventure—and it is your vocation. If you are a husband, if you are a father, then this is your divinely ordained path to personal greatness. Our vocation as husbands and fathers, though seeming to be common, mundane, and unexciting, is the very path that God has marked for you and me, in order that we may achieve our personal end, our glorious destiny.

The human father has been targeted and is being hunted by the evil one and his minions, but often he does not realize that he is being hunted, or why he is being hunted, because he does not comprehend his noble, powerful, divinely ordained identity. The enemy presses his insidious will upon the human father, relentlessly pursuing him, working tirelessly to submerge him under the tide of temptations, with the purpose of drowning his desire to discover his true identity and purpose. Why? Because the evil one knows that the human father has the power to change this fallen world, to lead his family from the shadowy jaws of death to the land of eternal light and bliss.

The enemy knows that if the human father assumes his divinely ordained charitable authority, the micro church of the family will be restored and revitalized, and these micro churches of the family will revive the universal Church, and the renewed Church will eventually convert the world. This is the epic battle of our time, and you and I are at the center of this confrontation between good and evil. The key to winning the battle is the human father—you and I. You are not the problem; indeed, you are the solution.

The longing for the Father is the deepest and most profound desire of the human heart. The apostle Philip, on the night before Jesus' ultimate act of sacrificial love, pleaded with his Lord, "[S]how us the Father, and we shall be satisfied" (John 14:8). Indeed, it is the vision of the Father that satisfies the human person's craving for validation, affirmation, and love.

Jesus' response to Philip is pivotal: "Do you not believe that I am in the Father and the Father is in me? The words that I say to you I do not speak on my own authority; but the Father who dwells in me does his works. Believe me that I am in the Father and the Father is in me" (John 14:10–11). Because of your baptism, Christ lives in you, and therefore you are capable of imaging the eternal Father to your children. Furthermore, because the Son of the Father became the son of a human father, all fathers have been made capable of imaging the eternal Father to their children. Philip's heartfelt desire is also the deepest longing of our children's hungry souls: "Show us the Father." This is our noble duty, our divine purpose, our call to glory— to show our children the Father. And this holy endeavor can only be accomplished by fulfilling the words of Christ, "I am in the Father and the Father is in me."

This book contains the battle plan: seven fundamental keys to becoming the father that God has created and destined you to be—a father who lives in the Father and has the Father living in him. It is now time for us to enter this battle, fully armed, with the bold commitment to sacrifice ourselves for our wives, children, and the future of humanity by becoming a father on earth like the Father in heaven.

SECRET 1

REDISCOVER FATHERHOOD

The Gaze That We All Desire

"Go with the pitch. Don't try to kill it or control it—just go with it." My dad wasn't a professional, but he knew how to hit a baseball. It was some of the best advice that an up-and-coming wannabe slugger could receive. Being a right-handed batter, my tendency was to take any pitch, regardless of where it was located, wrangle it, and launch it into left field—and hopefully over the left-field fence—but it never worked. I habitually attempted to corral and control the ball, making it do what I wanted, rather than moving with the ball and using its energy, motion, and placement to my advantage.

By high school I had learned how to "go with the pitch," taking a ball located on the outside corner of the plate to the opposite field. I enjoyed doing it, not only because it was an effective tactic and boosted my batting average, but because it made my dad proud.

I relished driving home with dad after a good batting performance and hearing him say things like, "Dev, you got a stick. I love how you went with that pitch and scratched out that double—that's how ya' win games." I craved his affirmation. It gave me strength, confidence, and delight, and it gave me hope—hope that I could really be something, that I could be great.

It was my sophomore year, early in the baseball season, when dad's advice would be of particular importance. Our opponents' pitcher had a cannon, and I couldn't swing my bat fast enough to connect with his fastball. My first couple of at bats were humiliating. Later in the game, with teammates on base, I was at bat once again. This was the type of clutch moment of which I had always dreamed. It was a do-or-die moment—and unfortunately I felt as though I was dying. I was nervous, but not only nervous, I was frustrated with myself. *Why wasn't I hitting this guy? What could I do to get my bat around quicker? What if I blow this?*

I backed up as far as legally possible within the batter's box in order to create more distance between myself and the pitcher, hoping that those extra couple of inches would give me the advantage I needed. But after a swing and a miss, it was obvious that another tactic was needed. I reset my stance, entrenched my cleats in the sand, and waited. The pitch came in like a rocket, a little high and a little outside. Without hesitation, I knew exactly what to do: "Go with the pitch." And so I did—and it was effective. I crushed it deep into right field. I could hardly take my eyes off that ball as I sprinted toward first base. It was my first home run—in fact, it was my only home run during the four years of my high school baseball career.

By the time I arrived at home plate, my teammates had lifted me on their shoulders, tossing me like a salad. It was glorious—the moment of which every young ballplayer dreams. But the glory and the moment were fleeting. While I was relishing the moment, I instinctively scanned the bleachers, searching the grandstands for something—for someone. I was looking for his gaze; I was searching for him —for my dad—but he wasn't there, he was at work; and even though I knew he wasn't there, I nevertheless strained in hopes that I'd find his face among those cheering fans. I was looking for my dad's approval—the attaboy, thumbs up, fist pump—telling me that he was proud of me.

It was my only home run, and I accomplished it by following his advice. How I wished that he could have seen me in that moment—that I could have had his approval —but he didn't witness my moment of glory.

What is it about dad? Why is it that when we purchase a vehicle we want dad to be the first to see it? Why is it that after we catch the big fish we feel the need to show him photos while recounting the tale? Why is it that after landing a job, bowling a 300, or finding the woman of our dreams, we want to share our success with him? There is a deeper motivation behind these actions than "I want to make him proud." *Why* do we want to make dad proud?

We look for his approval, for his eyes to rest on us with delight, because his gaze transmits and communicates something transcendent. Deep down, we long for dad's gaze because we desire His gaze—the Father's gaze. We desire our father's approval because we want to be approved of by the Father. We desire to be a chosen son because we want God to choose us as His son—and not just any son, but a chosen son in whom He delights.

The desire to be approved of, delighted in, and chosen is programmed into us; it is inherent in our being, and even from our earliest years we sense this need. A couple of years ago, my daughter, Zelie then six years old, decided to put on a dance performance for the family. She had been preparing for most of the day. She chose the perfect music, her favorite dress (the purple sparkly one), and practiced her routine several times. Acknowledging the importance of the occasion, her mother, four sisters, and I gave the event, and her, serious attention and focus.

As she danced, I could not help but notice the beauty of her fair skin, the shimmer of her golden hair—in a word, her innocence. I also noticed that, as she danced, she watched her feet with attentiveness and particular care in order to ensure that they did exactly what she intended, while occasionally, momentarily, looking up to make certain that all eyes were upon her.

I also perceived something else—something that moved me more deeply than her fair skin and golden hair, even more than her innocence. When she looked up to see if anyone was watching her, she consistently looked at me. Our eyes must have met over a dozen times. At first, it felt a little uncomfortable, but each time those twinkling silver-grey pools of shimmering light spoke to me, they transmitted a message that is the basis of everything important. Zelie was looking for her father's gaze. She wanted to know that I approved of her and delighted in her—that I loved her.

Zelie may have been looking for my gaze, but on a much deeper level, she was looking for the Father's gaze. I may have been scanning the bleachers for the face of my father, but in a more profound way, I was looking for my heavenly Father.

The Gaze of the Father

By means of one of the last prophecies uttered in the Old Testament, God transmitted His message of the necessity and vitality of fatherhood through the prophet Malachi: "Behold, I will send you Elijah the prophet before the great and awesome day of the Lord comes. And he will turn the hearts of fathers to their children and the hearts of children to their fathers, lest I come and strike the land with a curse" (Mal. 4:5–6).

By means of these words, the Father disclosed His heart's desire, His purpose and intention: God desires to turn the hearts of fathers to their children in order that the hearts of children will turn to their fathers. Why? Because if human fathers turn their gaze, their attention, and their focus upon their children, their children will not only see their own father anew, but begin to feel the gaze of their heavenly Father.

By confidently turning their hearts toward their earthly father, children will turn, with confidence, toward their Father in heaven. But if our daughters don't have our gaze of love and affection, they will search for that gaze of love and affirmation in a disordered manner from boys who are incapable of loving them truly. If our sons don't have our gaze of approval, they will seek approval from those of whom we do not approve. If our children do not have our gaze of love and delight, it will be gravely difficult for them to trust and believe that they have the Father's gaze.

The human father is a link between God the Father and His children. He is the voice of the Father that our children cannot hear, the face of the Father that our children cannot see, and the touch of the Father that our children cannot feel. It is vital that we fathers become this link between God and His children, for if we don't—as the prophet Malachi hints—the world will fall apart at the seams, crumble, and implode. This will not happen because God wills our destruction. On the contrary, He desires that all men be saved (1 Tim. 2:4). The world's demise will only occur because we have allowed it to occur.

God is giving us the plan to evade nuclear disaster: Fathers, if you love your children, they will not only love you, but will also experience God the Father's love.

But our world is falling apart—we are breaking, if not broken. Divorces are at an all-time high, while the rate of first-time marriages is at an all-time low. If you can believe the research, nearly half of children grow up in homes with half of their parents. Nearly half of Americans get married and a staggering number of those marriages end in divorce. We have an increased number of abortions and decreased population growth. We consume more and more, only to have emptier souls.

At the heart of nearly every major cultural moral crisis is the crisis of fatherhood. The statistics consistently and powerfully validate this point. When a father is absent physically or neglectful spiritually, the probability of children engaging in criminal activity, becoming incarcerated, becoming addicted to drugs and alcohol, using pornography, experiencing teenage pregnancies, dropping out of school, acquiring sexually transmitted diseases, eventually becoming divorced—all increase exponentially.

Society goes by way of the family, and the family goes by way of the father. If we want to change the world, we fathers must change. Hollywood and prime-time situation comedies have nearly convinced us that we don't matter, that we aren't needed, that a father is merely a sperm donor, and that our families and society are better off without us. Fatherhood, however, is like oxygen. Human beings cannot live without oxygen and society cannot survive without fathers. The evil one knows this, and this truth causes him to fear. God has ordained that fatherhood be a key transmitter of His salvation, and this should give us real hope. It is essential for the human father to understand and live this truth so that things can change for the better.

What Can One Man Do?

Regardless of the topic being discussed, whether it is partisan politics, third-world poverty and famine, tyrannical dictatorships, economic crises, interreligious conflict, the moral crises facing not only America but the world at large, inevitably someone will eventually say something like, "What's the matter with our world?" Or "How on earth did we get here?" And perhaps an even more important question: "How do we get out of this mess?" But when we begin to identify solutions to such pandemics and global dysfunction, we sense our helplessness and extreme insignificance and often end the conversation with the futile response: "What can one man do?"

This is a fair question. What can an unknown, 1-in-8-billion, average man with an average job and mediocre social media following do? It seems that most men believe that on their own they are ineffective and powerless, lacking the influence, personality, and talent to change society for the better. What is the result of this type of thinking? Instead of using our gifts, talents, and abilities for the purpose of making the world a better place, we numb ourselves with distractions that ease the pain and sense of mission, and eventually snuff out the still, small voice within us that calls us to personal greatness. We are tempted to believe the lie that we are nothing and can do nothing. We are tempted to believe that we can make little or no real difference, impact, or change. Although it is true that apart from Christ we can do nothing (John 15:5), we must always believe that with Christ all things are possible (Phil. 4:13). God does not call the qualified but rather qualifies the called. It matters little if you believe that you are not qualified to accomplish great things—you are still called to be a man of greatness, a great father.

While preparing for his ordination, St. John Vianney said to the rector of his major seminary, "Samson used a jawbone of an ass to slay a thousand Philistines. Imagine what you can do with an entire ass."[1] St. John Vianney was touching upon a core tenet of the Christian faith: God uses the weak to shame the proud. God used an ass to bring Jesus into Jerusalem. God "needs" you to father because our children need God the Father. God calls us fathers to be the ass that brings Him into His temple—the hearts of our family members.

The power to change the world exists within you and me. The questions regarding the world's dilemmas and successes, its destiny and glory, are inseparable from the fundamental questions about ourselves: "What is my identity?" "What is my destiny?" "What is the meaning and purpose of my life?" The world's destiny is profoundly connected to the human father's identity. My identity leads me to my destiny. Who I am determines who I will become. If I embrace and engage my fatherly identity, I become capable of leading my family to its destiny.

Laying the Foundation of Fatherhood

Several summers ago, I was given the noble duty of setting up the family pool in our backyard. The pool—a poor man's pool—aptly named the "Easy Set Pool," was an 18-foot-long round plastic sheet with an inflatable ring attached to the top of the liner. In just three simple steps —first, locate a level area onto which the liner should be laid; second, fill the inflatable ring with air; and third, fill the pool with water—voila! An instant summer paradise and a virtual babysitter with the potential to consume hours upon hours of our children's summer vacation.

How difficult could this project be? "Easy Set" says it all. I proceeded to survey the backyard, eyeballing what I considered to be the most level area of the yard, and set myself to the task. My children were delighted, itching with anticipation, clamoring for their first dip in our oasis.

The process was a cinch. In just a few hours, the pool was nearly ready for swimmers. When I examined it, however, I discovered that the waterline wasn't exactly level. What I mean by not exactly is that the water declined approximately a foot and a half from one side of the pool to the other side. Not bad if the pool is twelve-feet deep, but devastating for a pool with a three-foot water depth. Nevertheless, not having the guts to explain to the children that we should start over, I completed the water-filling phase.

It really wasn't as bad as I had originally surmised—it was worse. On the west side of the pool, the water level appeared to be at an appropriate height; however, on the east side, the water was nearly flowing over the inflatable rim. The endgame was in sight. With keen insight, I perceived the gravity of the situation: if enough water flowed over the east side, the east wall would certainly collapse.

Attempting to keep the dream alive, I explained the situation to the children: if they wanted their summer swimming experience to last, it was imperative that they stay away from that side of the pool. They nodded vigorously as, attired in goggles and flippers, and rafts in hand, they piled in. My wife acted as lifeguard, sitting in a lawn chair along the east side of the pool, while I stood along the opposite side with a sense of deep, personal, fatherly satisfaction. The kids were happy.

That is, until Gabby, my ten-year-old daughter, while performing her rendition of Huck Finn, began drifting on her raft toward the east side. As predicted, within milliseconds, the east wall of the pool collapsed, screaming ensued, and my daughter flew over the edge like a barrel over Niagara Falls. She was gone, and so was the water. My wife's eyes popped out of her skull (almost) as the deluge nearly swept her and her lawn chair away. The tide rushed full speed toward our shed, overtaking it and shaking it violently. All was lost.

That day, I learned a valuable lesson: whether the project is setting up a pool, building a house, or building a family, establishing a solid, level, balanced, secure, strong foundation is not only necessary, it is a prime factor in any successful endeavor. In fact, much like my pool project, our wives' and children's futures and happiness to a large extent depend on whether we build this foundation properly.

What is the foundation upon which we should build our families and society? And how do we ensure that it is solid and secure, balanced and level?

The world is populated by the human family, and God has established the Church as His visible family on earth —a family that is divinely ordained to be the herald of hope and transmitter of redemptive grace. It is this grace, transmitted by God's family, the Church, that is capable of healing our broken world. The family of God's Church is comprised of smaller family units, which are not only the fundamental cells of society, but also the very nucleus and heart of the Church. Families are created by marriages, and great marriages and great families typically have at their core a man who is willing to initiate self-donation, that is, willing to set the pace of self-giving love and to establish charitable authority—the divinely ordained authority to love by leading and to lead in love.

This reality is validated by the data. For example, the journal *Child Development* reported that teens who have involved fathers are less likely to engage in risky sexual activities, and although an involved mother can help to prevent teen sexual activity, fathers have twice the influence.[2] In terms of spiritual leadership at home, Focus on the Family noted, "If a mother is the first to become a

Christian in a household, there is a 17% probability that everyone in the household will follow. If the father is the first to become a Christian in a household, there is a 93% probability that everyone in the household will follow."[3] Furthermore, researchers at Columbia University found that children living in two-parent households who have poor relationships with their fathers are 68 percent more likely to smoke, drink, or use drugs, compared to all teens in two-parent households.[4] Teens in single-mother households fared much worse. They had a 30-percent higher risk than those in all two-parent households.[5]

From a human, pragmatic perspective, your fatherhood not only matters, it is foundational. You are vital, necessary, and essential to your children and their future. From a divine perspective, you are the link, the anchor, a transmitter of grace and salvation to your family. God the Father "needs" you to father, because your children need God the Father.

If the world is to be converted, the Church must be renewed. If the Church, the macro family of God, is to be renewed, the micro church—the family—must be restored and revitalized; and if the family is to be restored and revitalized, the man who is both husband and father must become a father on earth like the Father in heaven. The foundation of healthy, well-balanced societies, Church communities, and families is the human father. How he lays the foundation affects everything.

Identity Leads to Destiny

As mentioned above, our identity as men, as fathers, is deeply connected to the world's destiny. This is precisely why the enemy attempts to use intimidation, distraction, temptation, and eventual isolation as tactics to thwart us from becoming the men, husbands, and fathers that God has created us to be. The enemy works tirelessly to blind us from recognizing and recovering our true identity, and the very path that leads to that identity. Why? Because he knows something that we should also know: if we discover our identity we will most likely achieve our destiny, and assist our wives and children in achieving their destinies.

As a child, I spent countless hours manufacturing imaginary situations in which I was the slugger who, in the seventh game of the World Series, with two outs in the bottom of the ninth, three runs down, and an 0 and 2 count —and a nearly infinite amount of foul balls—blasted the game-winning grand slam. I was the Jedi warrior who saved Princess Leia from the grips of Darth Vader—even after my light saber was robbed from me. The hero lives deep in each one of us. But for most of us, we've sentenced him to an eternal time-out, subconsciously telling him that he can only come out and play after he matures and grows up (that is, after he becomes politically correct). And when he does come out to play, his desire for greatness has been neutered, castrated, mitigated, resented, and even, at times, rejected.

But God has created you and me with a true, authentic, relentless desire for greatness, and this greatness can only be achieved by becoming the person that God has created us to be. As St. Catherine of Siena said, "If you are what you should be, you will set the whole world ablaze."[6] But how do we become who we really are? How do we become who we have been created to be?

Our greatness is linked to our destiny, our destiny is connected to our identity, and our identity is discovered by means of our vocation. A vocation is more than an occupation. An occupation is what you do; a vocation is who you are. A carpenter is replaceable; a father is not.

St. Joseph's carpentry products no longer exist, but his fatherhood is eternal. We are first fathers and husbands. This authentically masculine fatherly identity, if embraced and followed, will lead us to our destiny. Our vocation as fathers is our path to greatness. By glorifying the heavenly Father with his fatherhood, the earthly father will be glorified by God the Father.

Pipes and Living Water

Nearly twenty years ago, my wife and I purchased a 1914 Arts and Crafts-style two-story home. It is my first and only home. I love this house. I hate this house. It has so much promise—the original custom woodwork, pillars, hardwood floors, and open layout. It has so many problems—too many to list here. My remodeling projects are continual and continually giving birth to more projects. My projects become problems and my problems create more projects. Not only is my house in need of repair, but my repairing skills need repairing.

Shortly after moving in to this promising, problem-infested cottage, I would, on occasion, discover a puddle of water in the center of the kitchen floor. Time and time again, I would examine the ceiling and find no evidence of a leak—not even water damage. The occurrence was sporadic, inconsistent, and elusive. Due to the fact that it never caused any apparent damage, it was easier to simply accept the problem rather than solve it. That is, until the morning that I stumbled groggy-eyed into the kitchen, and just before flipping the light switch, discovered that the plastic sheet that covered the ballast lighting was sagging like a belly of a pregnant cow. The light cavity was full of water, contained only by the plastic.

The time had arrived for me to determine the source of the leak. My first step was to shut off the electricity to the kitchen! Second, I speculated that because the second-floor bathroom was directly above the kitchen, there existed three possible causes of the dilemma: the toilet, the sink, or the bathtub.

We changed the toilet seal, the toilet flange, and eventually the toilet itself. The problem appeared to be fixed, until once again the puddle mysteriously appeared in the middle of the kitchen floor. We replaced the bathtub seal, replaced the sink, put new shut-off valves on the water supply lines, and even replaced the supply lines themselves.

The problem appeared to be resolved, until once again the insidious puddle appeared. We ripped out the bathroom walls to inspect the shower plumbing and eventually tore out the floor in hopes of locating a faulty pipe. Still, no remedy.

Finally, in complete desperation, I decided to tear out the kitchen ceiling. It was then that I discovered that the previous owner had put in a drop ceiling, no more than six inches below the preexisting ceiling. Hmmm. Now, why would they have done that? You know why—because it was a cover-up, a facade created to mask the real problem! Madder than the devil in heaven, I unleashed my rage as I removed and destroyed that drop ceiling. Sure enough, directly below the cast iron tub, which rested atop the floor joists above the kitchen, was the source of my lamentations. The drain line to the bathtub was slightly disconnected— and had been for years.

We can restructure our Church programs, be creative with our Catechism classes, tweak our liturgies, increase the number of Bible studies, provide more Church and community-outreach ministries, and establish another week-day "coffee clutcher," but in the end, the statistics confirm that regardless of how noble and good these things may be, they are a Band-Aid on a gaping wound. They are akin to changing the toilet flange when the tub drain is in need of repair. In fact, often we as a Church spin our wheels, spitting mud in every direction, spending more time, effort, and money on "solutions" that we believe will repair a problem, when a completely different remedy is needed.

It's time to remove the drop ceiling, the cover-up, the facade, and gain access to the leaky pipe. And just in case any clarification is needed: the pipe was not the problem; the connection was faulty. The problem is not fatherhood —it is fatherhood's connection with the Father that is in need of repair.

Fatherhood is the pipe that transmits the living waters of salvation to our children. Your fatherhood is a conduit that extends from heaven to earth, from God to man. You are a pipeline between heaven and earth, between God the Father and His children.

To be more precise, each of our vocations as fathers is a small pipe in a big pipeline system. To ensure that this pipeline of fatherhood is transmitting living water, it is imperative that we examine it and ensure that it is functioning properly. Only in this way can we offer our broken world living water. To accomplish this we will need to examine our connection—our connection to God the Father, Who connected Himself to us by means of a Son who had an earthly father, St. Joseph.

The Famine of Fatherhood

Remember the question: What can one man do? During the early history of the Israelites, Abraham's grandson Jacob begot twelve sons, one of whom was named Joseph. Joseph was the youngest of Jacob's sons, and his father's favorite, and because of this favor, his brothers grew exceedingly jealous of him and sold him to nomadic gum traders, who in turn sold him as a slave to the Egyptians. While in Egypt, in prison, Joseph was summoned to interpret Pharaoh's dream, which he interpreted accurately.

The dream prophetically foretold that the world would benefit from seven years of bountiful, fruitful harvest, which would subsequently be followed by seven years of famine.

Because of Joseph's successful interpretation of Pharaoh's dream, Pharaoh gave him authority over all of Egypt, and made him master over his household, second only to Pharaoh himself. During the seven years of plenty, Joseph had his people gather the grain and retain the harvest in the Egyptian storehouses in order to prepare for the foretold famine. When the famine struck the land, the inhabitants of the Middle-Eastern world turned to Egypt and its Pharaoh, who directed the people to "Go to Joseph; what he says to you, do" (Gen. 41:55). They obtained grain from Joseph, and from that grain made bread for themselves and their families, and thus were spared from starvation. God, through one man, saved the world from peril.

Today, much like the epoch of Joseph the patriarch, there exists a famine—the famine of fatherhood. Our wives and children, our Church and parish communities are starving for authentic leadership.

To whom should we turn to obtain the spiritual food needed to overcome this plight? To whom should we go to obtain spiritual bread in this season of need?

Recall the last divine utterance spoken in the Old Testament: "I will turn the hearts of fathers to the children and the hearts of children to their fathers" (Mal. 4:6). Fast forward to the New Testament, to the first time that God speaks to His people concerning His divine plan: God will "turn the hearts of the fathers to the children, and the disobedient to the wisdom of the just, to make ready for the Lord a people prepared" (Luke 1:17). The similarity is not only striking, but the connection is deliberate and loaded with rich meaning.

Notice that the first half of the message given by the angel Gabriel to Zachariah and recounted by Luke is the same as the divine utterance transmitted to Malachi: God will provide a special grace, a divine prompting, urging fathers to turn their gaze upon their children, in order that their children may experience the Father's gaze. However, the second half of the prophecy is altered with slightly different language: he will turn the hearts of the incredulous, that is, those who are rebellious and disbelieving, to the wisdom of the just. By connecting the two prophecies, we begin to understand that the incredulous are the disbelieving children whose hearts can be converted by turning toward the just.

But who is the just, wise, father from whom we fathers can learn how to become wise and just? The sacred text is obviously speaking directly of John the Baptist, but can also be interpreted as symbolically referring to someone else. Who is the just steward who will give to us men, who are starving for spiritual leadership, the very bread, the very Word of God that we need to give to our children? As Jesus put it: "Who then is the faithful and wise servant, whom his master has set over his household, to give them their food at the proper time? Blessed is that servant whom his master when he comes will find so doing. Truly, I say to you, he will set him over all his possessions" (Matt. 24:45).

Sacred Scripture attests that St. Joseph was a "just man" (Matt. 1:29) who was placed over the Master's household,

that is, over the Lord's family—Jesus and Mary—to serve
them by protecting, feeding, and teaching. In another parable of Jesus, the phrase "master over the household" is interpreted from the Latin text as "paterfamilias," or father
of the family. St. Joseph, the just, wise, and faithful steward, has not only been divinely ordained to be the "paterfamilias," the father of the Holy Family, but also was pro-
claimed by Pope Pius IX, on December 8, 1870, the patron
and protector of the universal Church. The word "patron"
is derived from the Latin root word "*pater*," meaning "father."

Recall that the macro Church is comprised of the micro
church of the family. If the Church is to become a holy
family it should be comprised of holy families who are
modeled after the Holy Family. If God deemed it fitting
that Joseph be the steward, patron, and father of the
archetype and model of the Church—the Holy Family—it
is only appropriate that he also be our spiritual patron, our
model, as well. In addition, God making St. Joseph the head
of the Holy Family also indicates that we fathers should
imitate St. Joseph and accept our charitable authority over
our households.

Go to Joseph

The Gospel of Matthew begins with the genealogy of
Jesus. The begats begin with Abraham, the first father,
our "father in faith" (Rom. 4:13–25, Hebrews 11:8), and
end with the last father, St. Joseph, the "just man" (Matt.
1:29) "who lives by faith" (Hab. 2:4, Heb. 10:38, Rom. 1:17).
By means of this profound connection between these two
just, faithful fathers, God is calling us to pay particular
attention to this "pipeline of fatherhood," which transmits
the living water of salvation in the person of Jesus Christ.

God has placed Joseph, son of Jacob, the final father in the list of the patriarchs, over the household of the Church with authority second only to God, with the purpose of obtaining for us the spiritual food necessary to overcome spiritual famine. In our age, God is saying, "Go to Joseph; what he says to you, do" (Gen. 41:55). What does the humble carpenter from Nazareth, of whom not a single word is recorded, tell us fathers to do?

Years ago, a dear friend of mine, now a priest, gave me an antique print of the *Flight into Egypt*—a depiction of Jesus, Mary, and Joseph fleeing from Herod and traveling the treacherous dirt roads down to Egypt. One evening, after the family went to bed, I studied the painting and as I meditated upon it I asked God, "Who am I in this scene? Am I Jesus, held securely and safely in Mary's embrace? Am I Mary, holding and protecting the Word incarnate —God made flesh? Am I the strong and resilient Joseph, who heroically leads Jesus and Mary to safety?" Just as I completed my pious musings, the solemn words came to me, "No, Devin. You are the ass." As one archbishop speaking to a large crowd of priests and seminarians once said, "God uses asses," and after pausing for effect, he continued, "because that is all he has to work with."

St. Joseph leads us fathers, us mules—who carry the precious treasures of Jesus and Mary, particularly in our own families—by the halter through this land of exile to wherever the heavenly Father desires. Again, God specializes in using asses to bring His Son into the temples of our wives and children.

God is calling fathers of this age to follow St. Joseph's lead and his heroic example, and to learn from his trials, his humiliations, and his successes—as a husband and father—how to become a great husband and a great father. Joseph's silence speaks profoundly of his sure, steady, secure fatherly example. His littleness reveals the very glory, power, and greatness of his fatherhood. And Joseph's hiddenness reveals the secrets of fatherhood that God calls each of us to imitate. By "going to Joseph," we will discover the essential secrets that made this humble, unknown carpenter the greatest, most revered, and honored father of all time.

What can one man do? By embracing his identity as husband of the Mother, and father of the Son, Joseph became the savior of the Savior, the teacher of the Teacher, the master of the Master, the king of the King of Kings; the one who fed bread to the bread of life, and from this bread we all received life. Joseph embraced his fatherly identity, which led his family to its ultimate destiny. Joseph's fatherly identity and example will be of great benefit to us who lead our families and this spiritually starving world to their destinies.

With God, one man can change the world. Joseph's fatherhood leads us to God's fatherhood, and following him we can become men who, by discovering our identity, change the course of history and achieve our destiny. Let us "go to Joseph" and learn from his timeless wisdom and ageless example the seven secrets to becoming a father of greatness.

Icon of God's Fatherhood

A "good ol' boy," a blue-collar entrepreneur with a rural bent, a mechanic of sorts, and a convincing salesman by nature, my father-in-law is—how shall we say it—an interesting man. Kenny can fix anything, except himself, and would much rather stick his hand in an engine with moving parts than ever have a dentist stick his fingers in his mouth. Hospitals and healers, nurses and needles, doctors and dentists put the fear of God into him.

Case in point: At an early age, due to tooth decay, Kenny lost nearly all of his teeth, and has donned dentures for the majority of his life. A couple of years ago, his latest set of dentures, which no longer fit properly, began to cause him severe gum pain. Sometimes he would call me on the phone and I would be convinced by his garbled speech that he was tanked, liquored up, drunk as a skunk.

"Kenny, I'm having difficulty understanding you," I'd say.

"Just a minute," he'd respond, giving himself a couple of seconds to reset his teeth. "How does that sound—better?"

The conversation would usually end with me attempting to convince him to visit the dentist and obtain a new set of dentures. After nearly a year of coaxing and explaining that dentists really are our friends, Kenny mustered enough courage to call a dentist and set an appointment. He explained his problem to the receptionist.

She asked him, "Sir, how long have you had the dentures?"

Kenny responded, "I think it's been over thirty years."

After a long pause, the receptionist replied, "Sir, that's a long time for a set of dentures."

My father-in-law—in classic Kenny style—responded, "You think that's bad? They were my father's before he gave them to me."

We inherit much from our fathers—some of which is good and some of which is not so good; I hope for most of us it is nothing quite as macabre as a pair of used dentures. It could be argued that the last several generations of fathers, through little fault of their own, inherited something worse than an overused, tea-stained set of dentures: we've inherited a lost vision of authentic masculine, godly fatherhood.

Many fathers have forgotten, or have never learned, what it means to be a father, how to father, or who we are actually fathering. Like a man who is unaware that the land he owns has a sizeable treasure buried just below the surface, often the human father neglects to reflect upon the power, necessity, and glory of his fatherhood. It is little wonder why atheism is on the rise. As our vision and understanding of the human father and his vital role diminishes, so, also, our vision and understanding of the heavenly Father vanishes.

Great fathers connect the world to the greatest Father. Our society desperately needs such men. But to become great fathers, it is imperative that we understand what a father is, what his essence is, what constitutes his identity. The human father has perhaps one of the most challenging jobs in the world—he is divinely ordained to be an icon, an efficacious—that is, a grace-transmitting—symbol of God the Father.

Near the end of my second year of college, I dropped my classes with the noble purpose of pursuing a promising career in retail. The career move was so successful that I would often trek home—under the pretense of becoming "reacquainted" with my parents—to wash my clothes and grab some real food, all gratis. It was during one of these visits that my dad asked me to come out to the porch and sit down with him. My father rarely asked me just to chat, and when he did, it was usually him chatting in a way that set me straight.

As dad sat down on the porch swing next to me, he unveiled a large-format, tabloid calendar and began flipping through several pages of impressive, impactful, illustrations created by some of the nation's best illustrators and graphic artists. It was somewhere near the middle of the calendar that he stopped turning the pages, set his index finger on the page, and said, "Dev, do you see this? I work for the father of the man who drew this. This guy pulls in 70K a year." 70K? I was tuned in; Dad was speaking my language. He turned his head and stared dead into my eyes, burning his intention into my soul, and said, "You're just as good as this guy—maybe even better. You've got the talent to be a great artist. You should quit wasting your talent and go to art school."

His words resonated in my soul. Like a hammer on the head, he'd nailed it. My father's encouragement set me on a completely different trajectory. Throughout my childhood, my mom told me that I had talent, entered my work in art shows; but it wasn't until dad stepped into the breach and spoke those words to me that I truly believed in myself and my God-given talent. For the last fifteen years, I have owned and operated a small branding and graphic design agency—all because of one man's encouragement.

What is the reason for that? What truth exists at the bottom of such an experience? The human father is called by God to be a link between his children and God the Father. The human father is the voice of the Father that his child cannot hear, the face of the Father that his child cannot see, the touch of the Father that his child cannot feel. *The human father is the visible icon of the heavenly Father*. This is not mere wishful thinking, pious idealism, or sentimental hopefulness: it is the divine plan. The divine word, the Sacred Scripture as articulated by St. Paul the Apostle, attests to this truth:

"For this cause I bow my knees to the Father of our Lord Jesus Christ, of whom all paternity in heaven and earth is named" (Eph. 3:14, Douay-Rheims). What this indicates is that the human father is named and claimed in the image of the eternal Father. A human father is called to be a father on earth like the Father in heaven, in order that his children who are on earth can hear, see, and touch the Father in heaven—through him.

We live in an iconic, brand-saturated world. Nearly everything and everyone has its own mark, its own symbol, its own logo that represents its meaning and mission, its product and purpose. Consider for a moment McDonald's golden arches. The McDonald's logo exists to direct us to the McDonald's franchise, and perhaps more directly, to a quarter pounder. The symbol, however, is not the reality, but merely an icon that reminds of and directs us to the reality of the restaurant.

Human fatherhood is a logo of the Logos, a pointer to the Pater. But unlike the McDonald's logo, or any logo for that matter, our fatherhood is animated by the very life of the Father, and therefore contains an element of the reality within it. This means that we are not the dads depicted as buffoons in television sitcoms. Rather, we are called to be like St. Joseph—icons of the heavenly Father, who transmit the very power and presence of the Pater. This is our identity.

Considering that the purpose of God becoming man— the Word becoming flesh in the person of Jesus—was to definitively reveal to humanity that God is our merciful Father; and considering that the divine mission is to turn the hearts of fathers to their children in order that children's hearts may be turned to their heavenly Father, we can begin to understand more clearly why Jesus desires for us to embrace and engage this iconic quality of fatherhood.

He said, "If you then, who are evil, know how to give good gifts to your children, how much more will your Father who is in heaven give good things to those who ask him!" (Matt. 7:11).

Our Lord invites us to consider the fact that even we fathers—though fallen, sinful, and selfish men—desire what is good for our children. But Jesus does not want us to simply stop our meditation there. He is calling us to make the connection in the comparison—to connect our limited desire for our children to receive good things with the heavenly Father's unlimited, eternal desire for our good. In other words, if we fathers want good things for our children, then God wants the *best* for His children.

This is why our iconic fatherly character is pivotal in our relationship with God. By meditating on the love we have for our own children, we discover more deeply how profoundly the Father loves, chooses, desires, and delights in each of us. Think about it: Why is it that a father would panic and yell at the top of his lungs while throwing himself between an oncoming bus and his three-year-old son? Because he loves him. Because he delights in him. Because he wants him to live, and to ensure that he does live, he is willing to die for him.

This is precisely how God loves you. He would much rather die in order that you may live—in fact, that is exactly what He did. God became a man, and allowed men to kill Him, to ensure that you, a man, might have His life, and have it abundantly—and believe in His love with abandonment and confidence.

Too many men walk around believing at some subconscious level that God doesn't desire them, that He neglects them, that He doesn't care. If God didn't care He would not have created you. Rather, He has given you life, and to prove that this gift is irrevocable, He has made the promise with, and in, His own body.

Our View of the Father Determines Our Fatherhood

"I'm a mess. My marriage is a wreck. I can't relate to my children. I don't know what to do." Bill, an apparently "happy," "nice," successful corporation owner, asked to meet for coffee. I expected the usual small talk, the hovering over the surface of topics, never discussing anything too personal. Today was different. Bill's facade, his world of illusion, was disappearing, and the inner man, the true man, who always wants to become who he is created to be, was fighting for life, for breath, struggling to come to the surface for air. After only ten minutes of conversation he confessed, in a moment of desperation, that he had struggled to be physically and verbally affectionate with his wife and children, and because of this his family was crumbling.

Bill had become aware that this type of affection was essential in the development of his children's character and his relationship with them, and was also discovering that his resistance to meeting their needs in this area was partly the cause of his family's recent implosion. What was preventing him from simply giving those he loved the physical affirmation they craved?

Later in the same conversation, Bill's eyes welled with tears as he told me that when he was four years old he had tried to kiss his father before going to sleep. His dad shunned him, saying that real men don't do that sort of thing.

Do what? Demonstrate their love for their children?

Bill confessed that he envisioned God as distant, unaffectionate, and cold—a God who expected results, rather than a Father who desires relationships. It's easy to connect the dots. Bill had projected the character of his father onto God the Father. But not only that. He had inherited this character, and had projected it onto his family. Bill's vision and understanding of the person of God the Father and His identity had shaped his own fatherhood.

Our vision, our understanding of God, shapes, forms, and determines our identity, our relationships, and the trajectory of our lives. If a man believes that God is a taskmaster, he will fear loving rather than love without fear. If a man believes that God is a taker, he will restrain his giving rather than give without restraint.

Everything regarding the human person—his character, his actions and thoughts—are the consequence of his lived response to this question: Do I trust that the Father loves me, and if so, to what degree?

This truth reminds me of the Parable of the Talents. The master departs on an extended journey and entrusts his wealth to three servants. To one he entrusts five talents, to another two talents, and to another a single talent. When Jesus lived on this earth, a talent was considered a large amount of money, equal to approximately 6,000 drachma or denarius, Greek or Roman silver coins. A denarius is believed by scholars to have been a Roman soldier's daily pay. In other words, the approximate worth of a single talent was 6,000 days' wages, or nineteen years' worth of salary.

Let's translate this into today's terms. Imagine a man earns a $50,000 annual salary. Multiply that salary by nineteen years, and you get the grand total of approximately $1 million. Not a bad salary for being at the right place at the right time. This indicates that the Master entrusted the first servant with an amount akin to $5 million, the second servant with $2 million, and the third servant received a measly $1 million.

Why is this information important? Because it testifies to an important truth: The Master is incredibly generous and entrusts His servants with much. This truth is the foundational premise of Jesus' parable, and this truth and how we respond to it determines our life story. God, symbolized by the master, is exceedingly generous.

We know the rest of the story. The master returns after his extended departure and settles accounts with his three servants. The first two servants traded, invested, and doubled their master's money and therefore were rewarded by being entrusted with even more riches, while the third servant, defined henceforth as the wicked and lazy servant, buried the talent and made no return on his master's investment. The dialogue between the master and the lazy servant, because of its ability to expose the mind of the wicked lazy servant, is worth quoting in full:

> He also who had received the one talent came forward, saying, "Master, I knew you to be a hard man, reaping where you did not sow, and gathering where you did not winnow; so I was afraid, and I went and hid your talent in the ground. Here you have what is yours." But his master answered him, "You wicked and slothful servant! You knew that I reap where I have not sowed, and gather where I have not winnowed? Then you ought to have invested my money with the bankers, and at my coming I should have received what was my own with interest. So take the talent from him, and give it to him who has the ten talents. For to every one who has, will more be given, and he will have abundance; but from him who has not, even what he has will be taken away. And cast the worthless servant into outer darkness; where there will be weeping and gnashing of teeth" (Matt. 25:24–30).

It stings, doesn't it? The account is simply uncomfortable to read. I always felt pity for the wicked and lazy servant. The master seems to be having a really bad day—perhaps his blood sugar levels were low—and the wicked servant received the brunt of his foul mood. But there's more to this story than a domineering, tyrannical master who blasts away at a helpless, fearful servant who lacks tenacity, courage, and financial wit.

Did you notice that the wicked servant's verbal description of the master was downright insulting? He used phrases such as "I know you to be a hard man," "reaping where you did not sow," "I was afraid . . ." Obviously this gent never read Dale Carnegie's book *How to Win Friends and Influence People*. The wicked servant believed his master to be harsh, selfish, cruel—a tyrant who uses people and takes from them what they do not even possess —and those characteristics paralyzed him with fear. Who wouldn't be afraid of a master like that?

But was the wicked servant's characterization of the master appropriate? Why did the other two servants double their master's money? Because they trusted the master and believed him to be generous—and He is. When was the last time someone entrusted you with a cool million?

Who we believe God to be determines who we are, and who we will become. Our vision of God determines the trajectory of our life. Do we view God as a competitor or a collaborator, as a pain or a partner? As a problem or a Pater?

Many men who are now fathers have been wounded deeply, perhaps by their own fathers, and those wounds may cut deep. The pain, the longing for authentic male affirmation, causes us to seek attention, glory, praise, and love in all sorts of disordered ways, with the aim and purpose of healing our insecurities. Many men wonder if they are real men, and not finding the right answer to that question, they recoil, hide the true man inside, and shrink away from sharing that true man—the talent that they have been given by the Master—with their children.

Investing in the Talent of the Child

Carol, a business acquaintance, has spent much time and effort consoling her friend Michelle. Michelle, who is in her sixties, and her husband, Robert, raised five beautiful, blond-haired, fair-skinned, blue-eyed daughters, who are all grown and have now moved into their own places. But those blue eyes have shades of gray—deep, sorrowful shades of gray. All the daughters, save one, have had multiple children by multiple fathers, and all these children were born out of wedlock. Three of the five daughters have drug addictions and several of them carry damaging sexually transmitted diseases. One of them has had five children with four different fathers, one of whom is in prison for sexually abusing her children. And only one of the five daughters attends church.

How did this happen? Carol said, "We used to wonder if Robert sexually molested his daughters. But that wasn't the case. He simply wasn't there. I mean, he was there—he existed, he breathed—but he wasn't there for his girls."

Robert didn't protect them when they were bullied. He didn't hug them or kiss them goodnight. He didn't tell them that they were beautiful or that he was proud of them. He didn't point out their talents or encourage them to become better. He didn't meet their boyfriends or help with homework. He simply didn't care.

And so, his daughters didn't care—for themselves.

Those beautiful daughters, who began life with innocence, laughter, eyes full of light, with a hopeful expectancy that a princess's dreams would one day be fulfilled, only grew colder, more cynical, and increasingly depressed as they sought the masculine affirmation, attention, and love that they did not receive from their dad in other boys trapped in men's bodies.

Carol's husband, Jim, stepped into this fatherless void and adopted three of Michelle's granddaughters. Jim literally saved those children from the hell that awaited them. Jim and Carol have paid a heavy price, and at times it has been trying, but nevertheless, they are a part of the healing process occurring in Michelle's granddaughters' lives.

What can one man do? One man saved those girls from an otherwise dead-end life.

Robert was given a lump full of talents and he buried every single one of them. The master returned and took some of them and gave them to Jim, who today is doing his part to ensure that those talents are not wasted.

The Master has entrusted every Father with His talents, that is, His children, and expects to receive them back with interest. It's nearly overwhelming to consider that God the Father entrusts His children to children who are fathers. But as in the Parable of the Talents, He "gives to each according to their ability."

If we are not vigilant regarding the health of our own souls, our insecurities and inferiority complexes will not only define us, but quite possibly define our children. Our identity determines our destiny and our understanding of God's identity determines our identity, which quite often affects our children's destiny.

Trusting in the Father

So, how do we obtain healing? Remember, man's vision of the Father determines his fatherhood. To become the father that you have been created to be, you must believe —regardless of your past—that the Father loves you and has deliberately chosen you to be His sign of fatherly love to this pained and wounded world. This demands that we trust in His love for us.

Trust is more than an intellectual assent to the truth that God exists. As St. James tells us in his very practical epistle, "Even the demons believe—and shudder" (James 2:19). Faith is not merely believing that a person exists, but trusting in that person. For example, I could be trapped on the rooftop of a building that is going down in flames. The firemen and EMTs arrive and extend a safety net and prompt me to plunge seven stories to safety. I can intellectually believe that the net exists, but unless I trust in the net and the men holding it, and jump into it, I will perish.

Trust is the essence of belief. Trust in God is the essence of our relationship with Him. So many of our ego-built, self-made lives are going down in flames. It is time for us to jump safely into the loving arms of a Father who desires the best for us.

Trust is the essence of sonship. The battle for sonship is each and every man's perennial battle to trust God as his father. To become a great father, one must first become a great son, and the essence of a great son is his trust in the greatest Father.

A friend of mine owned a beautiful cabin, tucked up in the southern California mountains. His father-in-law offered him a job that would immediately nearly double his income. He accepted the offer, sold his cabin, and moved his family across the United States and began his new job. After five months, the corporation lost its largest client and consequently my friend lost the job. He and his family trekked back to his hometown in southern California to live in an apartment that he referred to as a dump. About twice a month, he would trek up the winding road of that beautiful mountain to drive past the cabin that was once his.

Frustrated, pained, and feeling abandoned, he began to question God's fatherhood. "Why is it that just when I get my feet firmly planted, God has to pull the rug out from underneath me?"

Can we not all relate to his sentiments, at least a little bit?

Fifteen years ago, our third-oldest daughter, only a month after her birth, contracted RSV (respiratory syncytial virus). We readmitted her to the hospital and, due to the neglect of the hospital staff, she suffered a hypoxic event and permanent brain injury. Today she is disabled and confined to a wheelchair, and completely dependent upon others to perform the most basic functions. Shortly after that happened, I lost my job and had no way to pay the substantial hospital bills. And soon after *that* I was diagnosed with malignant cancer. I was having a bad week!

Why is it that God allows these things to happen? Does He gain great satisfaction from making our lives miserable and seeing us suffer? Is God against us? Does He take delight in punishing us?

Many men subconsciously believe that God is against them, or perhaps doesn't even care what happens to them. Is that the truth?

I believe that there is a deeper truth, one that if we embrace and engage will unlock the grace to live a life of greatness. The truth is that at the heart of every crisis, test, trial, and suffering is the intense battle to trust that God is Father—that He is your Father, my Father.

Precisely during a crisis, trial, or test we are tempted to doubt God's love for us. This is the evil one's tactic: to sow doubt in our minds and lead us to believe that God is not trustworthy. Doubt deflects God's grace, while trust unlocks His transformative, redemptive grace, which enables us to become manifestations of His glory.

So often, we have this idea that God is out to get us, but in light of His total self-gift this idea is simply illogical. Scripture promises us that "For with the LORD there is mercy, and with him is plenteous redemption" (Ps. 130:7). And "He who did not spare his own Son but gave him up for us all, will he not also give us all things with him?" (Rom. 8:32). And finally, Christ says to all of us, who are so plagued and burdened by the leprosy of our own sinful pasts, "Him who comes to me I will not cast out" (John 6:37).

God can heal our wounds of insecurity, feelings of inadequacy, and even our own failings because He has taken upon Himself our wounds—provided that we come to Him with those wounds and ask Him to heal us. Christ, on that cross, allowed Himself to feel abandoned by the Father, though he was never abandoned, so that you would know with absolute certainty that the Father will never abandon you.

Joseph's First Secret: Rediscover Your Vocation

The first secret to becoming a great father is to deliberately make the decision to embrace your vocation and identity as a father and understand that it is one of the most important things you will ever do. For some men, this may demand a physical return to their vocational post; for nearly all of us, this demands a mental and spiritual return—a rededication of ourselves to our mission.

We first encounter St. Joseph in Sacred Scripture amidst a vocational crisis, during his personal battle for sonship, his battle to trust in the Father.

Mary and Joseph were betrothed to one another, which in the ancient Jewish culture constituted the first stage of marriage. Mary and Joseph were married, yet according to the Jewish custom, were not to live together, or consummate their marriage, until after an extended waiting period. It was during this period of waiting that Mary was found pregnant, and upon Joseph's discovery of this reality, he fled from her, deciding to divorce her quietly (Matt. 1:29).

Joseph was withdrawing from his vocation, from his path to greatness, from his fatherly identity. But why?

So often, upon hearing this account of Joseph's dismissal of Mary, we think that he assumed that Mary had been unfaithful, that he had concluded from the evidence that Mary had committed adultery, and therefore, upholding his own purity, he left her. But there is more to the story.

It was during this marital stage of "waiting"—between the betrothal (the first stage of marriage) and the consummation, also known as the solemnization (the second stage of marriage)—that the angel Gabriel came to Mary with the divine message: "And behold, you will conceive in your womb and bear a son, and you shall call his name Jesus" (Luke 1:31). "And Mary said to the angel: 'How shall this be done, because I know not man?'" (Luke 1:34, Douay-Rheims).

At the time of the Annunciation, Mary was approximately thirteen to sixteen years of age. She was a young woman who understood how babies come into existence, for she said, "How shall this be done, because I know not man?" Mary was not a naive girl who lacked understanding of human sexuality and the one-flesh union. Based on this information, it would logically follow that Mary would have interpreted the angel's words "thou shall conceive" as indicating that "soon you shall reside with Joseph, and the two of you will consummate your marriage, and the fruit of this union will be the Son of the Most High."

But Mary's response indicates something entirely different. Mary's response presupposes that she has made a radical donation of herself and her virginity to God. This is why she said, "How shall this be done, because I know not man?"

Let's return to the question: Why did Joseph flee from Mary, his vocational post, and his call to greatness? Joseph knew Mary well. He knew of her holiness, her inner beauty, her faithfulness to and radical love for God. That is why he loved her and chose her to be his wife. And, as St. Thomas Aquinas and St. Augustine both contend, Joseph did not believe Mary to be guilty of adultery.[7] He fled for a different reason.

Joseph became fearful because in the presence of such a great mystery—a virgin pregnant with divine life (Isa. 7:14)—he sensed his own unworthiness. Mary is more than a regular woman. Mary is the New Ark of the Lord—the very dwelling place of God—and it is for this reason that Joseph was seized with holy fear.

In the Old Testament, the Ark is described as containing manna, the bread that fell from heaven in order to feed the Israelites while they wandered in the desert. The Ark also contained the Ten Commandments and the budded staff of Aaron, which symbolized the life of the Levitical priesthood, and was an instrument of Israel's redemption from slavery.

After the Ark was placed in the tent of meeting, the glory cloud, the sign of the very presence of God, overshadowed it and came upon it (Exod. 40:34).

Mary, the New Ark, contained within herself the fulfillment of the manna—the true bread from heaven—Jesus. She contained within herself the one who fulfilled the Ten Commandments, the Law, perfectly—the very Word of God Himself, Jesus. And living within the womb of Mary was the fulfillment of the Levitical priesthood, the great perfect high priest, Jesus Christ.

And if this is not enough evidence to convince us that Mary is the New Ark, Sacred Scripture states that the power of the Most High overshadowed her. The phrase used in the Greek to describe this act of overshadowing by the Holy Spirit is mentioned in Scripture in only one other place: when the glory cloud of God's presence hovered over the Ark in the tent of meeting.

Scripture tells us that David arose and went to the hill country of Judah to retrieve the Ark. After he attempted to bring it into Jerusalem, Uzzah stretched forth his hand to touch the Ark and was smote down on the spot, to which David responded, "How can I bring in the ark of God to me?" (1 Chron. 13:12, Douay-Rheims). Therefore the Ark remained in Obed-Edom the Gittite's house for three months.

Scripture also tells us that "Mary arose and went to the hill country of Judah to visit her kinswoman Elizabeth and that Elizabeth exclaimed, 'Who am I that the Mother of my Lord should come to me,'" and "Mary remained with Elizabeth for three months." In addition, the Greek word used to describe the action of Elizabeth, "exclaiming," was only used in the Old Testament to describe the praise that the Levitical priests gave to God before the Ark of the Lord.

What does all this indicate? Although Joseph was a "just man" (Matt. 1:29), he understood that he was unworthy of the Creator, the presence of God within Mary. Joseph's internal response could be summarized by the words: "Who am I that the Mother of the Lord should come to me?"

"Joseph, being a just man, and unwilling to expose Mary to shame, resolved to send her away quietly" (Matt. 1:19). The literal sense of the text is that Joseph was unwilling to expose Mary to the public shame of becoming pregnant by another man. However, one could also say that he was fearful of exposing Mary to his shame, that is, his potential to sin, and therefore dismissed himself.

In a certain sense, Joseph was intimidated by his vocation and because of this he withdrew.

But that's not the end of the story. God relentlessly pursued Joseph, calling him to heroically retrace his steps and recover and rediscover his vocational post and fulfill his calling of being the husband of the Mother of God, to ensure that he would also be a father of God's Son.

The message is clear: If God the Father chose a human father to be the father of the Son of God, then it is only logical that God deems fatherhood to be of the utmost importance. Just as God chose St. Joseph to be the human father of the Son of God, so also does God choose you, and in a certain qualified sense, "needs" you to become the father you are called to be. God "needs" you to father, because your children need God the Father.

By selecting Joseph to be the human father of the divine Son, God is stating that fatherhood is essential, vital, necessary, and a path to sainthood and glory.

As with Joseph, the evil one is determined to convince us that we are inadequate, incapable, unworthy, not great enough—or perhaps too great—to be the fathers that we are called to be.

Many of us sense that because of our sins, our past, and our shortcomings, we are not worthy to lead our families. Recall that of those who comprised the Holy Family, there were two perfect people: Mary and Jesus. Despite Joseph's limitations, he was called by God to protect, feed, and teach his family.

Regardless of how unworthy you and I may feel, God has deliberately chosen us for this mission. The road to personal greatness is before you. It is vital that we recover and rediscover the glory of our fatherly vocation. To embrace this great vocation, this path to glory, it is imperative that we trust the Father, believing that He can accomplish great things through our fatherhood. As with Joseph, God will give you and me the graces necessary to become a link between heaven and earth, an icon of God the Father—a father who leads his family to holiness and heaven.

SECRET 2

SET THE PACE OF
SELF-GIVING LOVE

The Desire for Glory

Among my immediate family members, I stand out as the
tallest. It should go without being said that a gift such
as height, though having tremendous advantages, should
never be a quality to boast about or to rub in another, perhaps shorter, person's face. To appreciate and revere such
a gift demands tact and delicacy. On one hand, someone
who is taller than others should not attempt to hide his
stature (as if he could) or diminish his presence, while on
the other hand, he shouldn't use a physical advantage such
as height in a domineering manner, with the purpose of
making others feel small.

I wasn't always the tallest person in my family. It took
many years to mature and reach this stature. In fact, when
I graduated high school I was 5'1.5", weighing in at a solid,
lean and mean 114 pounds. Today, I am a towering 5'7"
(I won't disclose my weight). Okay, so I am short—below
the average height of the adult United States male citizen
by 3.2"—but in Thailand I am a giant.

It's all perspective, it's all about how you look at things
—the glass is either half full or half empty. Even though
I was vertically challenged at 5'1.5" (in case you haven't

noticed, the half inch is extremely important to me), I was determined to play high school football. My mother was certain that I had a death wish.

What gives a young lad, whose nickname in junior high school was Keebler (fondly named after the cookie-making midget elf who lived in a small tree), the wild notion that he can actually compete with, hit, and tackle men literally twice his size? What incited King David, the young shepherd boy from Bethlehem (who was also short, by the way), to engage in battle against the super-giant, experienced warrior, man-killer Goliath?

Some time ago, as I was walking through my neighborhood, I came across a striking visual. A man was walking his beautiful, strong, sleek, black Labrador, while simultaneously a woman in a nearby house had allowed her little Yorkshire terrier outside to do his thing. As soon as this little Yorkie spotted the Lab, he became unglued—freaked out, as though there were an untamed lion condensed into a hamster's body. The Yorkie hurled itself headlong, full throttle, at the Lab and his master. The little tyrant yelped incessantly—with barely time to breathe in between barks —successfully guarding its domain from its enemy.

What was this dog thinking? That courageous, resilient, scrappy Yorkshire would have been blown off the lawn if that big, black Labrador so much as breathed in his direction.

There's something inside each of us, much like that little Yorkie, that compels us to believe that we are capable of being a defender, a protector—a man of heroic virtue. Deep within man, there exists a desire for battle, conquest, and adventure. At the foundation of these desires exists the authentic, properly ordered, desire for glory. All of us have been created by God to "obtain the glory of the Lord Jesus Christ" (2 Thes. 2:14). We've been created by God to glorify God, and by glorifying God we will be glorified. This dynamic of glorification is like the law of gravity. As creatures who live on earth, we are bound by gravity. God chooses to be bound by the law of supernatural love, and so when we glorify God, He cannot help Himself from glorifying us.

What does it mean to be a great man—a man of glory? What is the definition of a "real man"? What is the essence of the true man? Modern psychologists and evangelists tell us that the essence of a man is defined by being on an adventure, having a battle to fight, and having a beauty to win. Although it is true that most men, from childhood, desire adventures, envision themselves being engaged in battles, and dream of winning the beauty, these ideas— if acted upon or pursued without a proper context—can lead a man down a path that potentially jeopardizes his soul, his marriage, his life, his wife, and his family.

If being a real man is determined by whether he is on an adventure, entering battles, and winning beauties, then who determines the adventure, the battle, and the beauty? "There is a way that seems right to a man; but its end is the way to death" (Prov. 14:12).

There will always be higher cliffs from which to jump, taller mountains to climb, meaner men to fight, and more beautiful women to win; and even if we do achieve these objectives, they can only provide a false impression of self-confidence, that is, a confidence derived from ourselves. This type of self-made confidence is rooted in pride, and, as the saying goes, before the fall comes pride (Prov. 16:18).

And what happens to that self-made, bulletproof, impenetrable man when he fails? We've all been there.

Years ago, while I was employed as an art director for a local advertising agency, a project for which I was responsible printed incorrectly, and the mistake cost the agency a significant amount of money. My creative director, in front of the men on our creative team, gave me a satirical pat on the back while saying, "Go home and tell your wife that you're a failure." This was the same man who weeks before couldn't refrain from praising me for taking the lion's share of the regional annual advertising awards.

Most of us have had successes and failures. After the failures we tend to recount and replay the context and the conversations related to the event, then on the commute home, we begin to think, "If only I had said this," "If only I hadn't said that," "Why did I do this?" "Why did I do that?" Then the self-deprecating, self-emasculation process begins. We confirm our failure by telling ourselves that we are failures—that we really know that we are not "the man." And by the time we arrive home and the wife and the children—who depend on our strength—welcome us, we have very little left to give them.

Adventure, battles, and beauties are shifting sand upon which no man's identity can safely be built. There is a rock foundation that is more secure, strong, and stable —a foundation that will assist us men in attaining the fulfillment, greatness, and glory for which we long. The rock foundation is the context for the adventures, the battles, and the beauty; it is man's essence.

The Question of Essence

The question of essence is the essential question. The answer to life's most difficult questions—"Why am I here?" "Why do I exist?" "What is the purpose of my life?" "What is my destiny?"—can begin to be answered by understanding our identity—our essence.

St. John Paul II, in his *Theology of the Body*, explained that our mission, our reason for existence, and our destiny is etched in our very flesh. God has created the human body to reveal something of the mystery of God and to be a sign of His eternal love.[1]

Adam and Eve, in their very naked, pure, gloriously majestic bodies, revealed something of God's mystery and plan. Again, John Paul II says that, "Man becomes the image of God, not so much in the moment of solitude, as in the moment of communion."[2] This indicates that Adam's body and Eve's body—though capable of imaging God to some degree—make little sense by themselves, but rather, together, by means of their communion of persons —particularly in the one-flesh union—become capable of more fully imaging God.

How can this be? God is invisible, simple, and uncreated. Man, however, is created, visible, material, made with a body. Regardless of the vast abyss of difference between the Creator and the creature, between God and man, God wanted to span that gap and communicate to us His identity and our destiny. But how could a visible creature ever understand the mystery of an invisible God? It seems that God has a difficult task in communicating this reality to us carnal creatures. God did, however, provide a way that is tangible, real, and serves as a perpetual reminder to us of our identity and our destiny.

So what then is God's identity and what is our destiny and how are these realities communicated to us? "God has revealed his innermost secret: God himself is an eternal exchange of love, Father, Son, and Holy Spirit, and he has destined us to share in that exchange" (*Catechism of the Catholic Church* 221). The Trinity is an eternal exchange of Persons, an eternal exchange of self-giving love, and God desires that we partake eternally in this exchange of bliss, rapture, and ecstasy that will never end (CCC 1824).

God desired to communicate this eternal plan, our eternal destiny, to us by carving this message in our flesh.

Consider this: in order for the human race to survive, men and women must give themselves away to one another. God ordained this reality for the purpose of reminding us of His identity and our destiny—that we are made in His image of self-giving love, and that we will give ourselves away in love and we will receive God in love for all of eternity.

Man and woman, husband and wife, image God particularly when the two become one flesh and create another —a third. It is a reminder of the God who is love, the Son who is loved, and the love that comes forth from them, the Holy Spirit. The body, and the union between the sexes in the one-flesh union, has been divinely ordained to launch us into the very heart and mystery of God.

The human body reveals spiritual realities. The body expresses the deep, inner reality of the human person. A man's body indicates something about his mission. Although a man is made of the same substance as the woman—body and soul—his body indicates that he is fundamentally different from the woman. A man's body indicates that he is an initiator, a generator, that he goes forth from himself. This is a man's essence: he is divinely ordained to set the pace of self-giving love.

A man is principally, but not solely, responsible for the progress of this loving union between his wife and himself.

Two of the most notable examples of man's responsibility to set the pace of self-giving love are Adam, the first of all men, and the New Adam, Jesus Christ. The first Adam was given the responsibility to "till and keep" the garden. The Hebrew words for "till" and "keep" can be translated "to cherish" (*abad*) and "to protect" (*shamar*).

The word "garden" used in Sacred Scripture has both a literal and symbolic sense. The Garden of Eden was a literal place, but it also was a symbol of woman, that is, her interior mystery, her very person, her purity and innocence: "A garden locked is my sister, my bride, a garden locked, a fountain sealed" (Songs 4:12).

What does this indicate? This means that Adam was entrusted with the duty to cherish and protect the garden of Eve from shame.

We know the rest of the story—perhaps too well. Adam allowed the serpent to enter the garden and have his way with Eve—while he stood idle and watched. The consequence of Adam's neglect to protect his bride—to protect her garden—was sin, shame, blame, the disruption between the body and soul, and the rupture between the sexes throughout the ages.

The second example that demonstrates the responsibility for a man to set the pace of self-giving love is Jesus, the New Adam, who on the night that He was betrayed, rather than fleeing from the serpent, entered the garden and accepted responsibility for His bride, that is, for all of humanity, allowing her to escape the wrath that He endured on her behalf.

Both Adam and the New Adam exhibited self-donation, or absence thereof. The former established the paradigm of neglect, selfishness, and lust, while the latter set the paradigm of responsibility, selfless love, and pure self-donation.

From these two examples, we discover the second secret to becoming a great father, the deepest truth regarding man's essence: a man has been created by God to initiate and generate self-giving love for his bride and all women. This was his call in the beginning, and it remains his noble calling even today. Without experiencing this type of masculine sacrifice, a husband has not achieved manhood, nor is he fully alive.

Making Ideals Idols

Kyle was the type of friend with whom I was comfortable enough to debate for hours on end. Early in our friendship we would argue at length about religion, God, and the meaning of life. These weren't "nice-guy," sissified spats, but rather, red-faced, eye-popping, foaming at the mouth, practically choking the enemy type of verbal cage matches. Our discussions always ended the same way—with a strong, manly bear hug, a stinging slap on the back, and an agreement to be in disagreement.

He was faithful and I admired him. What wasn't to be admired? With a little scruff and grown-out hair, he was the spitting image of Aragorn from *The Return of the King*. With short hair, a leather jacket, and his motorcycle, he looked like James Dean. His wife, a blond-haired, blue-eyed, East Coast beauty, was his high school sweetheart. Kyle was the pastor of the largest, most popular youth movement in the region. With his locks, tattoos, a Harley, and the ability to play a mean electric guitar, he was a youth magnet. Kyle had it all—God, the girl, and good looks.

Kyle's ministry was synonymous with his adventure and his battle, and it was from this that he admitted he obtained his identity and self-confidence.

It was a Saturday afternoon when he called and asked me to meet with him privately at my office. His voice wasn't the typical deep, confident, strong one I was used to hearing; instead, his tone was somewhat soft and seemed to quiver a bit. I didn't ask any questions but obliged his request. I arrived in the parking lot first, and since it was a sunny spring day I decided to stand outside and wait. Within minutes Kyle cruised into the lot, Hollywood-style, on his motorcycle; he parked, dismounted, walked over to me, and suddenly grabbed onto my shoulders with both hands and buried his face in my chest and began to sob uncontrollably. I was stunned. What could make a man like Kyle crumble and fall into another man's arms like a little toddler who had fallen and scraped his knee?

It turned out that he fell into my arms because he *had* fallen.

Kyle had worked with a particular female volunteer for over five years. Though they interacted on a nearly daily basis, he had never been attracted to her or given her a second thought. But all that changed overnight, when she began sending very flattering e-mails.

He later confessed to me that, "She played on my hidden insecurities and my pride. Her comments got inside of me and hooked me. I found myself wanting to impress this person, and because of my insecurity and pride I became vulnerable. She would test the waters, take a big step, escalating the emotional grip, and then withdraw—only to ramp it up again. I was hooked. I became sucked into a cycle of infatuation and emotional thrill. I knew it was horribly wrong—so wrong—but I couldn't stop. It was weird; she wasn't the type that I was attracted to. It's not like she stepped out of a *Sports Illustrated* swimsuit issue. It was scary, because it was deeper than lust—she fed my craving for affirmation; she fed my insecurity by feeding my pride."

And the inevitable occurred—he fell in battle; he was wounded and nearly dead.

His mistress's husband discovered the affair, stopped by Kyle's house, and literally nearly killed him. Though he outlived the beating and the affair, his reputation didn't.

Kyle shared with me, "My entire identity was gone. I went from a most loved religious leader, to the person who everyone hated—even my wife hated me. I almost didn't survive. Anxiety took hold of me, incredibly paralyzing anxiety. It was touch and go—I could barely physically function. To this day I suffer from paranoia and anxiety. What I learned from this is that my identity was fake—I was fake. I lost everything. My image, my ministry—that was my battle—but I lost. I failed. What do you do when you fail?"

What was the key mistake? Kyle mistakenly made the ideal his idol. He himself determined the adventure—his ministry—and that adventure became his identity. And as long as the adventure was going on as planned, and the fruits of that adventure were confirmed by a female volunteer beauty, his identity was intact. Yet his adventure wasn't truly his essence or his identity.

Often we can dupe ourselves into believing that we have our eyes set on the correct target, when the target is actually a demonic decoy. Kyle's sights were set on his ideal, rather than on his essence, and it was his essence, that is, the divine call to set the pace of self-giving love, that was undermined.

Discovering Your Essence Amidst Crisis

The defining moment for every man is determined by how he responds to and endures his personal crisis. This is precisely where we encounter St. Joseph for the first time in Sacred Scripture—amidst a major personal crisis: his wife is pregnant without his cooperation.

Let's pause and reflect on this. Put yourself in Joseph's sandals. How would you or I respond to our beloved, our betrothed, arriving on the scene, three months pregnant without our involvement?

Joseph's response is pivotal and provides incredible insight into how we, as men, are called to set the pace of self-giving love. Scripture tells us that "Joseph, being a just man and unwilling to put her to shame, resolved to send her [Mary] away quietly" (Matt. 1:19).

The first vital lesson we learn from Joseph is that he did not cling to Mary—to woman—for validation, or depend upon her to determine his ultimate identity. Joseph didn't hold on to woman as a means of obtaining value. Joseph, rather, clung to God and placed his confidence in his heavenly Father. In other words, Joseph's identity was in his Creator and not in the creature.

The second lesson we learn from Joseph's example is just as crucial: Joseph refused to expose Mary to shame. But let's examine this. If Joseph left Mary alone and pregnant, she and her pregnancy would have been scrutinized by the local Nazarene villagers. Mary would have endured the shame, criticism, and judgments of her fellow neighbors without anyone to defend her. She certainly would have been exposed to shame.

But it could be said that Joseph was also fearful of exposing Mary to his own shame. How so? The verb "*degmatizo*," translated here as "expose her to shame," and "*apoulo*," translated as "divorce," can be translated as "But Joseph, her spouse, who was a just man, and who did not wish to unveil (her mystery), resolved to secretly separate himself from her."[3] Joseph did not wish to unveil the mystery of Mary to his potential to sin. He only desired to protect, to "*shamar*," Mary's garden from shame, and it was precisely because of Joseph's willingness to "*shamar*" Mary from all shame that he was chosen by God to "take her into his home."

How we respond to woman—whether by unveiling her, that is, unclothing her illicitly, even if only in our imagination, or by upholding her dignity as the ark of life—will determine our destiny. We can either set the paradigm of neglect like Adam, or the paradigm of self-giving love like the New Adam.

Kyle, reflecting upon the devastation and ruin that he caused his wife, said:

> When you see the person that you love the most de-stroyed, knowing that it is your fault—knowing that you inflicted her deepest wound—do you stick by her, or do you leave her? Most men leave, because they don't want to deal with the humiliation and the long, painful process of forgiveness. I decided to stick with her, and protect her. I was, and still am, determined to make her heart more important than mine. I never want to see her pained like that again. I'll die to my-self to become her protector—her protector from me, from pain. This means that I need to protect her from my harsh words, criticisms, and my actions.

So often, as men we desire to win the battle and the beauty only for the purpose of satiating our prideful long-ings. We fight from our strength as if we are really strong. What Kyle learned is that the real battle is not fought with our strength, but rather from our very weakness. If we fight from our strength, that is, our pride, we will even-tually fail.

So many men are afraid to admit their weaknesses because they believe that by admitting them, they become weak. Let's examine the logic behind this thought. I am short. But if I deny this reality, I will not be short. If I don't admit I'm short, but pretend that I am tall, I am actually tall.

If only this were true—but it's foolishness.

If I don't admit my weakness, my weakness nevertheless exists. Although I mask it with strength, that makes me even weaker, because by living in denial I never seek the strength that I need to overcome my weakness. So often, we bury the weakness beneath a facade of self-made strength, and then we shove this facade in the faces of the people around us, hoping to convince them of things that we ourselves aren't convinced of.

Our culture is saturated with this dynamic: men boasting of sexcapades, boasting of their robust Facebook followings, wearing T-shirts two sizes too small, all with the purpose of transmitting the message: Look at me, affirm me, can't you see that I'm a real man? We shove our desired image of ourselves in others' faces, hoping that they will be convinced that we are the man.

The battle must be fought from our weakness, for God's power is made perfect in weakness (2 Cor. 12:9). To become true men, we don't accept our sins and merely admit our weaknesses, but rather, admit our sins and embrace our weakness, or better still, embrace our weakness, and let Christ breathe His strength into that weakness. It is then, in that weakness, that Christ can be glorified in us. Why? Because when we admit our weaknesses and great things occur after our confession, we can only conclude that God accomplished these things—not us.

How we need to hear this message. We have all failed. If we haven't failed, then we are not in need of someone to save us from our failures. A savior can only save those who want and need to be saved. Jesus came for sinners, not for the self-righteous (Luke 5:32). Thanks be to God!

There is a greater need to minister to men who have failed than to those who have not, but, as Kyle says, "You don't simply put a sign on the church door that says,

'All men who have failed, welcome!' and expect guys to show up."

We receive woman by first doing what Joseph did, admitting our brokenness, our unworthiness, our weakness to God, lest we allow that unworthiness and brokenness to secretly dictate our behavior. If we do not admit our brokenness to God we may inadvertently break our wives and children.

Enter St. Joseph. Imagine, for a moment, Joseph's humiliation. He admits his limitations and surrenders the situation of Mary's pregnancy to God, and God calls him to retrace his steps and take up his post as defender, protector, and guardian of the Virgin. What would the villagers of Nazareth say? What scandal would Joseph have to endure? And yet, despite the humiliation he would incur, "he did as the angel of the Lord commanded" (Matt. 1:24).

The third vital lesson we learn from Joseph's heroic example is that the key to becoming great is to first become humble. Joseph's first step toward fatherly greatness was receiving the Woman, whose seed—Jesus—crushes Satan's head. Humility comes by means of Mary, and it is humility that crushes the evil one. To become a great father, we must receive the greatest Mother, and by receiving the Mother, we will truly receive the Son, the one who crushes the enemy of our manhood.

Consider that the Word's first step in saving man was entrusting His entire self to the Blessed Mother by becoming a helpless infant in her womb. The very flesh and blood that hung on the cross in the person of Jesus was donated by Mary. Our Lord completely entrusted His entire mission to Mary. At the foot of the cross, Our Lord commanded the beloved disciple John to "Behold your Mother," and from that moment, he entrusted himself to her. But do you know who entrusted Himself first to Mary, before all of these? God the Father did. God the Father entrusted His most precious gift, His very Son, to a human woman.

St. Joseph, being an icon of God the Father, imitated the Father by entrusting his mission to Mary, and by doing so, he became a great husband and father—if not the greatest. If it's good enough for the Father, the Son, John the Evangelist, and St. Joseph, it is certainly good enough for me.

The beginning of Joseph's incredible vocation was inaugurated by his reception of Mary into his home and into his heart. Our vocations as husbands and fathers will only be great if we humble ourselves by receiving Mary, and set the pace of self-giving love for our wives and children.

But what does it mean to receive woman? To father in the image of God the Father, we "husband" in the image of Christ. We are called to unite ourselves to our brides as Christ united Himself to His Church. By doing so, we become capable of becoming great fathers.

It is difficult to set the pace of self-giving love in our marriages. Our marriages will undergo moments of duress, resentments, bitter battles, division, and implosion—at least that's what my friends tell me. It is during these moments that we must remain yoked to our wives.

A yoke is a mechanism of restraint that is placed over the neck of a beast of burden. The yoke is attached to cords or rope that are attached to a load. Often two oxen or two animals were yoked together, and the synergy between the two beasts would pull far more than their combined pull weight. When we remain yoked to our wives and bear their burdens as our own, we are able, as a couple, to pull far more of the family's burdens than if we were to attempt to do so by ourselves.

I like to imagine myself as the leper in the Gospel account, who was healed by Christ. I'm very thankful but I go my merry way. After returning to my village and being welcomed by my family, I open up a shop in downtown Jerusalem.

One day, while working in my shop, I hear the clamor of a large crowd, shouting and screaming as they fill the dusty streets of Jerusalem. As I step outside my shop and into the wild throng I ask the man next to me what the reason is for the ruckus and he responds, "That Jesus of Nazareth . . . they are taking him to Calvary to be crucified." His words seize me. I realize that I have only this one last opportunity to thank Him for healing me of my leprosy.

I launch out after Him, determined to see Him, determined to thank Him one last time. I weave my way through the multitudes, pushing, pulling—just trying to find a way to reach Him. Finally, at the foot of Calvary the crowd thins, and I gain front-row access just at the moment when they strip Him of His clothing. And then I see it for the first time—His body, plagued with open sores, eaten by the scourges, lacerations, and infected wounds. And then I understand: in order for Jesus to heal me of my leprosy He took upon Himself my wounds, my leprosy.

The key to setting the pace of self-giving love within marriage and healing our wives of their wounds is bearing their wounds as our own. We must never give up on our wives. Perhaps a qualifier is needed. You may be divorced and it is impossible for you to return to your wife. Recently, I encountered an old friend whose wife had five affairs with five different men while he and she were married. He became bitter, resentful, and overwhelmed with a deep-seated hatred for her. It had been a year and half since their divorce. I asked him how he was doing and he responded that he was doing extremely well. When I asked what was the secret to his newfound peace, he told me, "I stopped resenting her, started to forgive her, and pray for her every day."

His children actually told him that they said to their mother, "Mom, why do you run dad down all the time? He never talks bad about you." This is a man who understands his goal: to help his wife and children arrive in the Fatherland. This is a man who sets the pace of self-giving love.

Our wives are not the load; they are not the burden; they are not the enemy. We share their burdens as our own by not resenting, always forgiving, and praying for them daily.

A man who sets the pace of self-giving love chooses not to wound his wife, but rather to bear her burdens as his own, and in doing so he refuses to be the enemy and becomes a source of healing.

The Enemy Inside

Toward the end of what could be considered a perfect spring day (the one and only nice day in Iowa's calendar), I decided to walk to my local parish church, about a half a mile from home. While I was there, the groundskeeper, Dan, walked in and said that a tornado had been spotted just south of town and was moving in our direction.

Remembering that two of my daughters were home alone, I immediately vacated the premises and began sprinting home. The bright spring sky had been replaced by an ominous skyscape, which included a mass of towering clouds moving like a freight train in my direction. Though alarmed and overwhelmed, I had a single objective: to get home to ensure that my girls were safe.

It was one thing to sprint a half mile in my Kenneth Coles; it was quite another when sheet after sheet of rain began to assail me. Beset by both the rain and violent winds, I felt as though I was running in place. At one point, the wind became so violent that I was forced to grab onto a nearby tree and hug it to maintain standing. I must have looked ridiculous. While being intimate with that tree, I realized how truly helpless I was against such a powerful enemy.

At that moment, my biggest enemy was that tornado. It had the potential to devastate and destroy my children, my home, and my life. Although it was a tremendously destructive enemy, capable of permanently damaging everything I cared about, I have a larger, perhaps even more ominous enemy, who has the potential to rob my wife and children of joy, peace, and vitality. That enemy is me.

On the one hand, I can be my family's greatest advocate, but on the other hand, if I don't master my passions, I can be their worst enemy.

It is easy to believe the lie that our personal life and private actions do not affect our children. However, our interior life gives our exterior life form. Who we are on the inside determines who we are on the outside. Our interior sexual posture—even if we attempt to conceal it —does affect our children's sexual attitudes, mores, and behaviors.

A friend of mine, Don, after nursing a secret porn addiction for nearly two decades, was caught by his employer viewing pornography on his work computer. That night he confessed his addiction to his wife, but no other members of their family were made aware of Don's problem. Don, his wife, and their children were pillars in their church community. Several of his daughters were leaders in their parish's youth group. Shortly after Don's admission to his wife, his daughter confessed to him that she may have an

STD, and that she was pregnant and wasn't certain who the father of the child was.

Truly, we cannot give what we do not have. If we have love, we are capable of giving love; if we are bound by lust, we are capable of transmitting that evil—an evil that will also bind our children.

Lust will be allowed to conquer us, and our families, if we attempt to conquer women by means of our lusts. Lust attempts to divorce love from sacrifice. In other words, lust attempts to keep us from obtaining our identity: men who set the pace of self-giving love, men who give themselves away for the sake of the other. If we give, we live; if we use, we will lose. Lust attempts to chain a man in boyhood.

For example, after a fourteen-year hiatus, my old college buddy Rick and I were able to connect via telephone. During the conversation, he mentioned that he was about to celebrate his fortieth birthday. I congratulated him with a couple of wisecracks about wearing adult diapers and suspenders. Following the chuckling there was a prolonged pause. Rick finally broke the silence, hesitated, and then reluctantly confessed that although he was turning forty he still felt like he was a boy.

What plagued Rick plagues most of us. The sickness, the cancer that hollows out the soul and infects the marrow of the spirit of a man is lust. Rick was addicted to lust, to pornography, to idolizing and demeaning woman. But what caused him to lust? Rick sought validity, comfort, and a power that he did not possess, and the easy way to obtain those things was to objectify women—particularly women who don't fight back. By doing so, it wasn't necessary for him to sacrifice himself to be gratified. Yet, in the end, the gratification led to desolation. The valued "feeling" of being a man that he derived from his addiction to pornography chained him in boyhood, and his true identity as a man ever eluded him.

Often, when we are insecure, feeling inadequate, unsure of our identity, we can fall into the trap of seeking validation in what we think will make us manly, only to have it rob us of our very manhood.

John Paul II said that liberation of the heart from lust and the freedom it affords is "the condition of all life together in the truth."[4] If we want the vibrancy of Christ's resurrected life, and we want to obtain the truth of our identity, if we want to be free to love without self-preoccupation, it is imperative that we become liberated from lust. This, however, does not mean that we will be liberated from temptation. Rather, as St. Augustine says, "We work out our salvation by means of temptations."[5]

Responding to Sexual Temptations

God gives us the freedom to choose how we will pursue happiness in life. He does not coerce us into loving Him (which is the true and only happiness), but rather invites us to embrace true joy. The moment of decision for good or for evil, for triumph or for failure, for happiness or devastating sorrow, exists within the moment of temptation. How we respond to sexual temptations, in particular, tremendously impacts our lives. So how do we respond? What is the proper response?

We discover the ideal way of dealing with such temptations in the account in which our Lord was questioned about the adulterous woman. At dawn, the Pharisees apprehended a woman who had just been caught in the act of committing adultery, and dragged her, scantily clad, to the Temple, where Jesus was teaching. According to the

Law of Moses, such a woman ought to be stoned to death, lest her sin come upon the entire community.

The dilemma presented to Jesus was this: If He obeyed the Mosaic law and condemned the adulterous woman, He would betray His message of mercy; but by not obeying the law of Moses, He would be excusing her sin.

Unfortunately, most of us have been trained to believe that when faced with the temptation of lust, we have two options: to resist the temptation by condemning the woman, or by simply excusing her. So often, we internally condemn a woman for her immodesty, blaming her lack of respect for herself as the reason we objectify her. By condemning her, we condemn ourselves. On the other hand, we can excuse with the purpose to use. We excuse her behavior or her immodest attire, and by doing so, we submit to the temptation to, at some level, objectify her—to use her with the purpose of gratifying our disordered appetites.

When presented with this quandary, Jesus stooped down and began to write upon the ground. He then stood and said those most famous words, "Let him who is without sin among you be the first to throw a stone at her" (John 8:7). Jesus then stooped down a second time and continued writing on the ground. He stood again, and released the adulterous woman.

Since the first time I heard this account, I wondered, "What on earth was Jesus doing by writing in the sand?" Jesus' actions, each of them, have tremendous significance. One possible interpretation is that Jesus' first act of stooping down symbolizes His Incarnation, His condescension, His becoming like men, born from the dust of the earth. The word "Adam" means "from the earth." Jesus, the Word, became the New Adam, by condescending to the earth in order to "rewrite" salvation history in our very dust.

Our Lord then rose to defend the woman, whereas the first Adam did not. He then stooped again, symbolizing His death and burial in the earth, and His rising a second time signifies His Resurrection—His power to forgive, his power to release the woman. Truly, the one without sin, Jesus, cast the first stone on the morn of Resurrection Sunday, when He rolled away that stone from the opening of the tomb in order that His resurrected power could empower man to love rightly.

While the first Adam complied with the first woman who tempted him, the New Adam did not excuse the woman's sin or condemn her, but rather, released her.

What is the point of all of this? Jesus' actions reveal the key to defeating lust in the heart: when presented with sexual temptations, we should avoid condemning, complying with, or excusing the woman, but rather, we should release the woman to God.

This can be accomplished by first admitting the beauty of woman and thanking and praising God for this beauty. It truly is worthy of praise! Second, we must admit to God that we have failed in seeing that beauty correctly, that we've used that beauty selfishly for our own gratification. Third, we must admit that we are weak and cannot, of our own accord, see woman the way that God sees her —in all purity. Fourth, we must ask God to provide the power of His Resurrection—the Holy Spirit—the same power that definitively defeated sin and death and rolled away the stone from that tomb, the resurrected power that can remove the stone that eclipses the door to our hearts, so that we may become manifestations of His glory.

How do we receive this redemptive grace necessary to defeat lust in the heart? There is an answer: every man needs to have an accountability partner—but not just any accountability partner. You and I, we need the accountability partner par excellence—Jesus Christ. The key, or at least one of the most powerful keys, to defeating lust in the heart is attending and participating in daily Holy Mass. Why? Even if we fail, even if we falter and succumb to the temptations to lust by means of viewing pornography, masturbating, using contraception, having a physical or an emotional affair, desiring our neighbor's wife, we remain steadfast and persevere in attending Holy Mass. Though our sins weigh us down with tremendous guilt, and though we may be unable to receive the Lord's Body and Blood, the Eucharist, nevertheless, we approach the priest during Holy Communion, folding our arms across our chest as a gesture to plead for God's blessing.

Why is this important? By receiving the blessing, we humble ourselves before the Lord, admitting that we are unworthy to receive His holy Body and Blood. By humbling ourselves in this manner, God will eventually exalt us with the redemptive grace we need to defeat the demon of lust. As St. Peter said, "Humble yourselves therefore under the mighty hand of God, that in due time he may exalt you" (1 Pet. 5:6).

In addition to this, it is necessary to receive absolution by confessing our sins and then attending Holy Mass and receiving the Eucharist—the same Body and Blood of Jesus that defeated sin and death in His body, the same body that rose from the dead and defeated sin and death definitively.

At Holy Mass, precisely during Holy Communion, an incredible exchange occurs. Christ gives us Himself, the True Man, and the ability to defeat sin and death, and we give Him ourselves, our sins, and our potential. This moment is the culmination of many moments in which we release and surrender all temptations, doubts, and tendencies toward sin and receive the power to become a man of glory.

Temptation and Salvation

The Sea of Galilee is the largest below-sea-level freshwater lake on earth. It teems with life because the Jordan River flows in and out of it, circulating and recirculating its waters. The Dead Sea, on the other hand, receives water from the Jordan River, but it has no outlet. Therefore, its salt content is approximately 35 percent—that's nearly ten times more salt concentration than the ocean has.

In fact, the Dead Sea's salt concentration is so rich that it cannot support life.

In the context of sexual attraction, relationships with women, and working online, we will be bombarded by sexual temptations. Keep in mind that the temptation is not sin; it is only when we engage the temptation and begin to choose it that it becomes sinful. Nevertheless, as these thoughts bombard us, we will become extremely vulnerable to such temptations if our relationship with our wives is in crisis at any level.

By suppressing these temptations, by keeping them "inside of us," or by condemning the beauty of women, we will become increasingly tormented by such sexual temptations, and could eventually surrender the battle and give in. All of this can lead to the death of the soul, and by default be transmitted to our families.

But if we release the woman and our temptations to God, and offer to Him our weaknesses and our struggles as a sacrifice, we allow God to transform our work, our struggles, our water into wine—into grace—for ourselves and for our family.

When we fail to offer such temptations to God and cave in under the heavy weight of these thoughts, we sin. Now, sin is a reality that is not spoken of much these days. The word "sin" is derived from the Greek word that archers used for missing the mark. When missing the mark, Greek archers "sinned." We all sin, we all miss the mark. But what is the mark?

The mark is our destiny—eternal communion and union with the only One who can fulfill us—God. When we sin, we look for our destiny—that eternal union with God—in other places, which only leads to misery. Communion is the remedy for lust, and by overcoming lust we live in communion with God and our wives.

Crisis in our marriages and sexual temptations can be the proving ground for love and can afford us the opportunity to live in union with God if we operate like the Sea of Galilee and allow them to flow out from us and into God. Only God can transform our temptation into a means of salvation.

You and I are called to live from our masculine essence, to set the pace of self-giving love. This is the path to authentic manhood. This is the context for the adventure, the battle, and winning the beauty.

The secret to living from our essence—to becoming a true man—is to receive the true Woman, Mary. She is the New Ark, and was Joseph's secret weapon, and the very means by which he received the humility that made him great. To become great men, it is imperative that we entrust ourselves to the greatest Woman.

To become great fathers we need the greatest Mother. To become men of glory who set the pace of self-giving love for our women, we need the Woman who will obtain for us humility and the purity necessary to fulfill this mission.

The Ultimate Conquest

Not all temptations for husbands come from outside of one's marriage. If we're honest with ourselves, we need to acknowledge that we also battle temptations within marriage. Therefore, if you desire to be truly one with your wife and experience authentic unity with her, you ought to strive with all your intellect, will, and passions to love your wife in a disinterested manner.

By being disinterested, a husband strives with his entire being, both soul and body, to diminish all self-interest, redirecting all interest toward pleasing God and pleasing his wife. Indeed, the husband, by means of his actions and affections, must bear witness through his body that his wife's needs deserve his tender attention, and that his desire for pleasure can never come at the expense of his wife's dignity.

A husband's disordered self-interest, especially expressed within the marital act, will, over time, erode and numb his wife's sensitivity to her husband's advances. If this occurs, even selfless acts of affection offered by the husband will more likely be interpreted by the wife as an appeal for self-gratification at her expense.

If a husband's self-interest intensifies, becoming a relentless desire for self-gratification, the husband and wife will begin to separate interiorly; and if this separation, in its early stage, is not checked, the distance between the two will become a measurable gulf that will divorce the two in spirit. Eventually, this spiritual distance will become a fissure into which the unsupported family will fall.

Indeed your wife will inevitably view herself through your intentions. If your intentions are selfish, driven by lust, and impure, your wife will gradually view herself as an object to be used by her husband, rather than a person worthy of love.

Men are created with an innate desire to conquer, and often this desire to conquer is naturally, although erroneously,

transferred to women and marriage. The husband, however, who "conquers his wife" by means of lust has already
been conquered by his lusts. Let there be no doubt that lust
must be conquered or lust will conquer your marriage. Indeed, your wife is to be loved, not conquered, and to love,
lust must be conquered.

SECRET 3

SPIRITUALLY ADOPT
YOUR CHILDREN

A Father's Defining Moment

Children love Christmas. Why shouldn't they? It's the time of the year when they can submit ridiculous wish lists to the big man at the North Pole, understanding that there is a strong probability that they will receive what they ardently desire.

It was through this lens that, as a child, I understood Christmas as a season of great hope and expectation. I hoped and certainly expected that I would receive the gifts I wanted. My ninth Christmas was the year that I asked, pleaded, and begged for an Intellivision. (I'm really showing my age.) An Intellivision was a lot like Atari, a video gaming system that could entertain a young lad for weeks at a time—of course, accounting for bathroom breaks.

As Christmas drew near, ever more beautifully clad presents adorned the base of our Christmas tree. Each time presents were added, shuffled, and rearranged, I would evaluate the holiday landscape, hoping to find a present similar in size and weight to an Intellivision (touching the gifts was only "allowed" when dad and mom weren't present). With only a few days remaining before Christmas Day, the anticipated gift appeared. From that moment onward, that box was in my crosshairs. I could not stop daydreaming, considering the countless hours of fun that awaited.

Christmas Day arrived, and dad and mom waited until all the other gifts were opened before they revealed the "big gift." Mom would usually increase the anticipation by acting as though she had no recollection of the gift, or to whom it belonged. She would say something like, "I guess that's it, kids . . . Oh wait, there's one more present . . . Let's see who this one's for."

Like a ravaged beast devouring its prey, I ripped the skin off the package. Suddenly, to my horror and disbelief, I discovered that I had been duped—I had been given a game of Monopoly. It was cruel. In my mind, the act could have been considered child abuse. Could my parents be that sick?

Life can be like that. Our hearts may have been set on something that we have long desired, only to see the fulfillment of that desire vanish before our eyes. This reality also can apply to our children, and to our acceptance of the person that God has given us in that child.

Some dads, from the moment they see the positive sign on the pregnancy test, dream of having a boy, or a girl, a football star, or a princess. The options and aspirations are endless. But what happens when the father who desires a son, and expects a son, receives a daughter? What happens when the football player ends up being a pianist? Or worse, what happens when the oft-voiced prayer, "I don't care what sex it is, so long as it's healthy," is answered with a Down syndrome baby?

It is moments such as these that define our fatherhood and to a great extent shape our children's lives. How we receive and embrace and continually receive and embrace our children for who they are determines what kind of father we will be.

Rejecting or not accepting a child at any level can have potentially devastating consequences. A young child who has been rejected is not capable of comprehending the severity of the damage done to its soul, as he or she is not yet mature enough to understand. So the child represses the hurt, the pain, and the anger, and learns to cope with being less wanted and less loved. By acting in this way, the child's spark of hope for greatness, the joyful innocence of aspiring toward God and glory wane.

Why? Unlike an adult who, by grace, has discovered his identity or is in the process of discovering his identity and can fight against the lie of rejection, a child's identity is not solidified and therefore the child allows the rejection to define him.

Consider your own personal experience. We all want to be chosen, selected, needed, wanted, liked. Not just liked —loved, admired, and important. But for many of us, that hope has been diminished nearly altogether. We've been stigmatized and scandalized into believing that the real world is insensitive, hard, competitive. This belief consequently influences us to think that resilience and cold, calculated competitiveness are the essential characteristics of a human being who survives and succeeds. But, as many a man has experienced, resilience and competitiveness do not always instill confidence.

Being rejected and not accepted at an early age cuts deep into the human soul. The child who has been wounded in this manner attempts to cover the wound by manufacturing coping mechanisms, alter egos, pseudo personalities, in order to protect himself from being rejected again. The child thinks, "Nobody likes or wants the real me. I will fix that by becoming someone else—someone who is attractive, likeable, and wanted."

Hence, a girl adorns herself in overdone makeup at an early age or the boy creates stories of female conquest to make himself "respected" among his peers. The types of coping mechanisms are endless. In fact, if not checked, they won't end. Satan consistently returns with the dagger of insecurity to pierce the skin of the soul and aggravate the wound, while convincing the child that he is not good enough. The evil one's intention is never to allow the wound to heal. The more the enemy is allowed to keep the wound from healing, the more the person becomes someone he is not; and he eventually loses his true identity —the very identity that directs him to his destiny.

Unfortunately, many children receive this wound first-hand from their parents and sometimes just from their father. Such a wound can often demand a healing process that endures a lifetime. Research demonstrates that as authentic involved fatherhood diminishes, atheism increases.[1] Initially, that may appear to be very depressing news. However, if we reverse the statements, we discover that as fathers become more involved in their children's lives, belief in God increases. In other words, by turning our gaze—that is, our attention—upon our children, they will turn toward their Father in heaven.

So, what instills confidence in a child? A father who assures his child that he is wanted, chosen, accepted, and delighted in instills in the child tremendous confidence.

Biological and Spiritual Fatherhood

Fatherhood is not merely or essentially biological. Any man can be a biological dad, but it takes a real man to be a spiritual father. Consider that a man can plant his seed and leave the garden of woman. Though he is a biological father, he has abandoned the child, and that child will struggle from that point on to overcome this deficit. As mentioned earlier, the probabilities of children becoming convicts, having teenage pregnancies, acquiring sexually transmitted diseases, and having addictions, all increase dramatically when they come from fatherless homes.

How do we move beyond being merely biological, status quo dads to become intimate, attentive, engaged fathers? Our Lord gives us the answer: "Whoever receives one such child in my name receives me; and whoever receives me, receives not me but him who sent me" (Mark 9:37). These words, on the surface, may not appear to mean very much, but by peering deeper into them, we discover an essential truth regarding fatherhood.

When we receive a child as Christ, we not only receive Christ and the Father in the child, but the child will also be more likely to receive Christ from his or her father.

Receptivity is never a passive action, but rather an active one. A bride receives her husband, and receiving him, she gives herself in return. If she merely lives with him, she is "putting up with" him but not engaging him. Similarly, when God gives us a child, we don't merely live with the child as though we "put up with" the child for the next eighteen years, but rather, we receive the child's entire self as a gift from God and actively engage the child.

When a father actively receives his child, he is not only receiving the child, he is also receiving Christ in the child. As a priest friend of mine says regarding this truth, this elevates the child to a nearly eucharistic status. On a practical level, it prompts us fathers to peer beyond our children's epidermis and look deep into their souls—to see them as Christs. But it also means that we not only see them as Christs, but also as Jesus the child, the Babe, who became completely dependent upon human beings to raise Him.

When You Get What You Don't Expect

Thirteen years ago, I was out doing some last-minute Christmas shopping when I received a call from my wife telling me that she was going into labor. Normally, I would have been overwhelmed with excitement, but this, our third baby, was only in the twenty-eighth week of gestation. Thanks to an emergency cesarean section and a month of care in the neo-natal intensive care unit, our daughter, Anna Marie, survived.

She was incredibly small. Her entire body fit inside a baby Santa hat, and her little head was no larger than the size of a small apple. As I shared earlier, we brought her home, and after several days she contracted RSV, a cold that, by attacking a premature infant's lungs, had the potential to take her life.

We admitted her to the regular pediatric unit at the local hospital. The nurses, however, lacked the skill and experience necessary to care for her. Due to their neglect and hours of undetected apnea, our Anna Marie suffered a hypoxic event, in which not enough oxygen was transmitted to her brain. The medivac life-support team arrived and stabilized her, then transported her by helicopter to a major children's hospital approximately two hours from our home. By the time Anna Marie arrived there, she had had three clinical death experiences. The doctors and nurses worked tirelessly to save her life, but by the end of the traumatic episode, my daughter's brain was severely and permanently damaged.

I was overwhelmed. The situation was far too difficult to comprehend—or to accept. Our little Anna Marie, whose life had so much promise, had become someone I believed she was not intended to be. I denied the reality of her condition. We met with specialist after specialist who explained that our daughter was not going to have a normal life. I became defensive, enraged, and even argued passionately with some of these professionals, while disbelieving all of them. I simply could not believe the fact that Anna Marie would not recover.

I began to tell myself that those doctors and nurses stole my daughter from me. I simply could not accept what had happened, which in turn meant that I was not accepting Anna Marie for who she had become. Perhaps, on the surface, I accepted her in a passive manner—because I had to—but I didn't actively receive her, as I would receive Christ.

My brother-in-law, a very wealthy man, counseled me to take legal action against the hospital and offered to cover any legal expenses. It was an open-and-shut case: as the medivac team rolled my daughter on a gurney across the tarmac to the helicopter, the head nurse admitted that Anna Marie's condition was a result of their negligence. I needed some time to consider the matter. But the more I thought about suing the hospital, the angrier I became, and the angrier I became, the more my resentment toward Anna Marie began to mount.

At one point, I broke down, emotionally collapsing before God, begging for insight and guidance. It was then that this thought occurred to me: "Devin, if you do not forgive them, you will never accept Anna Marie for who she is."

Forgive them? Are you kidding? They robbed me of my daughter! They robbed her of a normal, functioning life!

I refused to surrender to God and forgive the nurses, and all the while I became further entrenched in my bitterness and resentment. Finally, in desperation, desiring that the cloud of despair would dissipate, I did something that to this day can only be credited to the grace of God: I called the head nurse and forgave her and her team for failing to care of Anna Marie.

The healing wasn't instantaneous, but I immediately decided that the child I had been given was not an accident or a substitute for the former Anna Marie, but was my child, the child that God chose to be the instrument to save me. By receiving Christ in the person of Anna Marie, I discovered an incredible truth: It was not I who needed to save Anna Marie, but rather, I who needed Anna Marie to save me.

And she has.

Today, Anna Marie is fourteen years old, imprisoned in a wheelchair, and, with severe cerebral palsy, labeled a "special-needs" child (don't we all have special needs!).

But she really is special. She is my anchor. I will be feeding her, changing her diapers, giving her baths, and transferring her from her bed to her chair and her chair to her bed, for as long as she or I live. She has taught me how to love, how to serve—how to set the pace of self-giving love. And by receiving Anna Marie, that is, by spiritually adopting her, I have received Christ and Anna has received Christ from me. I wanted an Intellivision— but instead I won the lottery. Does this mean that I'm an expert at self-donation? Far from it. I often struggle to be a sincere gift but that is precisely why I need Anna Marie: she compels me to serve.

Raising a Child Raises a Father

Meditating upon the reality of the Word becoming flesh from a divine perspective can be somewhat alarming. God the Father entrusted His most precious gift, His perfect Son, to a limited man, expecting him to be His Son's father.

Wasn't God afraid that Joseph would taint Jesus, or at the very least, misguide Him a time or two?

In the divine plan, God allowed Joseph to teach the Teacher and by doing so Joseph was taught by his son. Doesn't this occur to every father who receives his child as though he is Christ? The child serves as a means to transform the human father into a godly man. Raising a child raises a father. Upon having children, we, as fathers, begin to view the world through their eyes—through their innocence. Suddenly, the trip to the grocery store is longer in order to take the route that does not pass the Hooters billboard. The busiest lane at the grocery store becomes the optimal choice because its newsstand doesn't have *Cosmopolitan*. The television shows that we watch suddenly become more family friendly. Why is this? Because, as reflected through my child's innocent big blue eyes, the world that I thought I knew—that I believed to be harmless—will never look the same.

St. Joseph, as an icon of God the Father, spiritually adopted Jesus, a child not biologically his own. Joseph's example teaches us that to be a father means that we become a logo of the Logos, an iconic father of the heavenly Father. As God the Father has spiritually adopted us, and as St. Joseph spiritually adopted Jesus, we need to spiritually adopt our children. God the Father chose a human father to be the father of God the Son, because God the Son needed a human father. God needs us to be great fathers because our children need the greatest Father. Spiritual adoption is perhaps one of the most challenging yet rewarding jobs known to man.

Why can this duty be so difficult to fulfill? Well, frankly, because we don't know what we are doing! Often imperfect people make the mistake of trying to raise perfect kids. Imperfect people cannot raise perfect kids. Our children, like my Anna Marie, are not perfect, and even if they were perfect, they would still be the cause of much of our anguish.

Joseph's Son was perfect. Jesus was sinless. Yet, from day one of betrothing himself to Mary, the life of Joseph became a succession of intense events, containing within themselves multiple crises that shaped his fatherhood, his very identity.

Consider that if Joseph did not retrace his steps and return to Mary and remain her husband, she, according to the law of Moses, would have most likely been stoned to death. By shielding Mary, Joseph by default shielded the child in her womb. This cost him dearly. Joseph's reputation as a just and righteous Jew came under the scrutiny of his neighbors. Joseph became a protector.

Soon afterward, Mary and Joseph trekked to Bethlehem to be numbered among Caesar's census, but when they arrived, Mary entered into labor. Since there was no room for them in the inn, Joseph located a nearby cave, a manger within a rock, as a place for his wife to give birth to the Savior. By doing this, Joseph became a provider.

Soon, Herod, Judea's king, discovered that the promised Messiah King had been born, and instead of paying Him homage he viewed the child as his rival, a threat to his reign, and deployed his armies to murder Him. In the darkness of the night, Joseph fled with his wife and child to Egypt, a foreign land, whose inhabitants spoke a language that he did not know. It was there, in this land of exile, that Joseph employed himself to provide for his family. Joseph protected and provided.

Then there is the account of the events in the Temple. Joseph and Mary took the twelve-year-old Jesus to the Temple in Jerusalem to celebrate the feast of the Passover. Yet when the family departed for home, Jesus remained behind without His parents being aware of it. After a day's journey, Mary and Joseph could not find Jesus among the traveling company. What did Joseph feel?

Anguish. Guilt. Fear. Sorrow.

How could he not feel this way? He took his eyes off Jesus, he lost his Son. Seeing that Mary's heart was tortured by the loss, Joseph was determined to do all in his power to find the child and return Him to his Mother. Certainly, Joseph questioned his fatherhood, his ability to protect, provide for, and teach his child.

After three exhausting days of searching, Joseph most likely discovered an incredible truth: it was not Jesus who was lost without Joseph, but rather it was Joseph who was lost without Jesus. It was not Joseph who needed to save Jesus, but rather it was Jesus and His presence that saved Joseph.

Finally, after incredible personal anguish, Joseph's eyes rested upon his Son, the one who gave his life meaning. And though Jesus was in the Temple "doing His Father's business," He nevertheless went down with Mary and Joseph and remained obedient to them, and by doing this, Jesus allowed Joseph to become His teacher.

Though Jesus was perfect, raising Him caused Joseph tremendous anguish and pain. To spiritually adopt our children demands that we protect, feed, and teach them as Joseph protected, fed, and taught Jesus. Doing so isn't easy. In fact, being a father who protects, provides, and teaches can involve heroic sacrifice, and yet be most rewarding.

Perhaps one of the greatest challenges posed by spiritually adopting our children is that they are not perfect and they are not what we expected.

Charitable Authority: To Protect, Feed, and Teach

Fatherhood is not as much biological as it is spiritual. Fatherhood can be theological, but it should also be practical. What practical actions can a father implement after he has made the decision to spiritually adopt his child?

My father's oft-repeated words come to mind: "There are too many chiefs and not enough Indians," which can be translated to mean that if there is no one to lead, no one will follow. A leader must lead his family from wrong, or wrong will lead his family.

Nearly every successful initiative, institution, corporation, and apostolate has a person who has assumed the vital position of leader. Corporations are usually anchored by CEOs, businesses are operated by managers, sports teams follow their coaches, parishes are shepherded by priests, and families are led by fathers. Now, it may be somewhat politically incorrect to identify the father as the leader of his family, but let's face it, if he's not the leader, then who is?

Satan has nearly convinced fathers that their authority over the family is no different than that of mothers, and that fathers have no right to act in a leading manner, for by doing so, they are depriving mothers of equal dignity. Equality, however, does not mean an eradication of distinct characters and roles. What do I mean?

The Trinity, for example, is one eternal essence, and yet three distinct persons. The Father is a greater Father than the Son and the Son is a greater Son than the Father. Each is equal in essence and dignity, yet distinctly unique in role and person. The enemy has nearly convinced the human father that he has no unique, divinely instituted role in the family, and that he is merely a parent among parents, without a distinct character that distinguishes him from his wife.

The enemy has used this tactic to debilitate fathers, to induce them with a spiritual amnesia about their true identity, in order to render them weak, ashamed of their masculinity, and virtually ineffective.

Our Lord, confirming the vitality of a leader said, "I will strike the shepherd, and the sheep of the flock will be scattered" (Matt. 26:31). That could also be said this way: Strike the father and the family will fall, if not altogether fail.

What, then, is authority? What is charitable authority? *Webster's Dictionary* defines the word "authority" as "having control or the power to control," but that is not the original meaning of the word. The word "authority" originated in the twelfth century and is derived from the Latin word "*auctoritas*," which actually is derived from the word "*auctor*," or author, which means "to originate, create, write, to invent, influence, and command." The word "charity" is derived from the Latin word "*caritas*," and can be interpreted as "to value, esteem, to love," what we call agape, which is selfless, sacrificial, unconditional love, the highest of the four types of love in the Bible. In other words, charitable authority is the human father's divinely ordained role to write, to create, to influence the story written in his family's life by loving sacrificially. It is our responsibility as fathers and husbands to write the story of love and salvation in our wives' and children's lives. Modernism posited that there was and is no story, and that if a story exists, it must be destroyed. In a sense, modernism sought to destroy patriarchal authority. Moral theologian Janet Smith stated that "When fatherhood is absent from society you are left with chaos."[2] If we fathers do not lead we are not loving. We love by leading and lead by loving. Fatherhood is the distinct, divinely ordained role to lead. This role does not deny the equal dignity between spouses, but rather testifies to that equal dignity. In other words, male headship upholds female queenship.

If we fathers do not assume our position of charitable authority, we allow our families to become susceptible to many insidious temptations that will eventually deteriorate the familial bond and order of our families. If we choose not to exercise charitable authority over our family, we are choosing not to protect, feed, and teach—we are choosing not to serve. By denying our God-given authority over our families, we are granting the evil one the ability to rule and destroy our families.

Jesus alludes to this when He asks, "[H]ow can one enter a strong man's house and plunder his goods, unless he first binds the strong man? Then indeed he may plunder his house" (Matt. 12:29).

To plunder a house, the strong man of the house must first be rendered powerless, and then after he is bound, his possessions can be plundered. Though our Lord was specifically referring to His binding of Satan, this comparison can be applied to the human father.

The enemy is intent on binding us in order to minimize the power and effectiveness of our fatherhood. Satan desires to plunder our house in order to have his way with our wives and children. How does he do this? He uses three simple tactics to keep us from protecting, feeding, and teaching: intimidation, distraction, and temptation, which lead to eventual isolation.

Notice that the duties of protecting, feeding, and teaching are ways through which a father serves his family, and to serve in this manner presupposes the need for a father to exercise his God-given charitable authority—to love by leading and lead by loving.

Just in case you are not convinced that God has given you a divine calling to be a father who leads, consider

St. Joseph. Precisely by God becoming the "son of Joseph" (John 6:42), and God the Son being obedient unto him, God has exalted Joseph as the paradigm of all familial leadership. God appointed Joseph as "Lord of his house, and ruler of all his possessions" (Ps. 105:21). By appointing Joseph as ruler of His house, over His Son, God emphasizes the responsibility placed upon each and every father to fulfill his mission to serve by exercising his authority to protect, feed, and teach his family.

If the Blessed Mother, who is full of grace, and Jesus, who is full of grace and truth, submitted to the authority of Joseph, should not all fathers believe that they have been given similar authority over their families? Joseph was, by the holiness standard, not as qualified to lead as the other members of his family. But as mentioned earlier, God does not call the qualified; he qualifies the called.

Even if a father perceives that his wife and children are more worthy than himself, he should keep St. Joseph's fatherly authority as his model.

The Mountain of Sacrifice

In ancient cultural traditions, a name had tremendous significance. A name not only indicated an identity but also a purpose, perhaps even a divine mission. For example, Moses means "drawn from water." Moses, as a baby, was drawn out of a river by the Pharaoh's daughter, and because of that event, received a name that identified him and his mission. Later, God called Moses to lead the Israelites, dry shod, through the Red Sea in order to escape Pharaoh and his armies. God drew Moses and the Israelites "through water" to safety and victory.

Or consider Abraham, whose name means "father of many." Ironically, Abraham lacked an heir, the fruit of his loins, until the ripe old age of one hundred. Abraham's name indicated his identity and his identity indicated a crisis. Abraham embraced the crisis of not having an heir while believing that God would eventually provide him with a son—which God did.

The name Jacob meant "usurper," and it was Jacob who stole his brother's blessing by duping his blind father, Isaac, into believing that he was his older brother, Esau. Names have meanings and meanings have names.

I have the privilege of knowing a man who everyone refers to as Scott, but I will forever call him Maximus. Maximus Decimus Meridius was the commander of the Armies of the North, a military hero in the 2000 British-American epic historical drama *Gladiator*, who sacrificed his life for the sake of the Roman Republic.

Late last summer, Scott and his family were vacationing with their in-laws in upstate New York. According to their tradition, the adults and children who were old enough would caravan from the cabin where they lodged, through the dense pine forests, to a tucked-away hidden lake—a virtual private summer oasis. After a full day of swimming at the lake, the group began the return trek to the cabin. The rain that season saturated much of the woodlands, causing some of the lower-level trails to be washed out and unsuitable for hiking.

Forced to take the high trail, the caravan of four-wheelers skirted along a precipice while driving uphill. Scott, on his own four-wheeler, was following his college-aged daughter, Haley, who was driving her own four-wheeler, with her younger brother, Jer, on the back.

At the top of the hill, the front wheels of Haley's four-wheeler became lodged between several tree roots. She attempted to accelerate the vehicle slightly, but the ATV didn't budge. Since she was still on the up-side of a steep incline, with the precipice to her right, she became a bit unnerved and quickly hit the gas, bucking the four-wheeler, causing it to stand vertically, almost motionless, then slowly beginning to descend backward down the hill.

Haley and Jer had been hurled from the ATV just a stretch down the hillside, directly in the path of the ATV's backward fall. In what could only have been a millisecond, while the four-wheeler momentarily remained in its vertical position, Scott realized that all five hundred pounds of this sports utility vehicle was poised to fall directly on Haley and Jer.

Scott immediately jumped from his ATV, launched himself up the hill, and threw his body at Haley's four-wheeler —which had now begun to fall backward—giving it a full body block that would have stunned any NFL lineman. The hit was just enough to set the trajectory of the falling ATV inches to the right of his two children. Scott stood in the breach, took the hit—or literally laid the hit on the four-wheeler—in his effort to save his children's lives, understanding full well that there existed a great possibility of the four-wheeler crushing him. Hence the name Maximus.

Scott did what every man would hope to have the courage and determination to do—protect his loved ones by sacrificing himself, if needed.

There are indicators that alert us whether we are training ourselves to walk down this sacrificial path. By becoming acquainted with Scott over the years, I have discovered that his actions that saved his children's lives were the fruit of years of dying to himself in many and varied little ways.

When Scott was in college, his buddies were having premarital sex. Scott fell in love, and rather than succumbing to the temptation to do what his friends were doing, he

proposed to the woman he loved and waited to have inter-
course with her until they were married. Being married in
college demanded that Scott and his wife live off campus
in a mobile home, and make significant sacrifices to scrape
by. They began having children, and while his buddies
played with women without admitting any responsibility,
obtained their degrees, and landed their dream jobs, Scott
became a father, remained faithful to his wife, and surren-
dered his childhood dream of being a wilderness adventure
guide to work for social services in order to provide for
his new family.

Over the years, Scott gave up hobbies, career advances,
his material wants, and his personal desires so that his wife
and family could be protected, fed, and led.

Scott recounted to me a phone conversation in which
an old hiking comrade, after nearly two decades, caught
up with him and asked what he was doing professionally.
Scott confessed to me that he was ashamed to admit that
he worked behind a computer counting beans. As the tears
welled in his eyes, he related, "My friend said, 'Not you,
Scott—a desk job! We all thought you'd be somewhere in
the Sahara, or up north in Alaska, or in the Amazon—
not in an office.'"

Now let's step back and evaluate this. Most men, who
believe that life consists of being on an adventure, in a
battle, and winning the beauty, would lean back, scratch
their head, and say something like, "See, he gave up his
dreams, and look at the pain it causes him. He's dying a
slow death. He needs to cut the ball and chain."

But Scott realized that there is something deeper, that
he has an essence that compels him to set the pace of self-
giving love and live for his wife and family to ensure that
they may have life, and have it to the full.

It's ironic. Scott's family and his marriage is nothing less than admirable. He has lived the adventure, entered the battle, and won his beauty. All of this was accomplished by his setting the pace of self-giving love.

Many men sit around the campfire, smoking cigars and drinking whiskey, talking about what they're going to do —the palace that one day they will build; the mountains that they will one day climb. But that one day never seems to come because there never seems to be enough time in one day. And so the project of building the palace diminishes into little more than wishful thinking.

The secret to building the palace is placing one single rock upon another, each and every day. Little works, accomplished consistently over time, eventually become towering citadels. One scales a mountain step by step, not by leaping from the base to the peak.

By protecting our children and wives in the little and seemingly unnoticeable ways, day after day, year after year, we eventually scale the mountain of sacrifice, arriving at the peak of the mountain upon which we are willing to die.

Satan's Three Tactics

Recall that after King Herod discovered that the King of the Jews had been born in Bethlehem, he decided to have the child murdered. Joseph, after being warned in a dream by an angel that Herod was plotting to murder Jesus, fled with the child and Mary, veiled by night, to the foreign land of Egypt. Joseph's example becomes an allegory for all fatherhood. Herod, who symbolizes Satan, attempts to destroy the child—our children. Joseph symbolizes all fathers who protect their children and their children's mother by fleeing in the night. His night flight further symbolizes the hidden, secret care and protection of the human father by which the family is saved—even in Egypt —even in this world of exile.

Like Joseph, we are called to protect our wives and children from the Herods of our age. But who are the Herods of our age, from whom we should protect our children? Generally speaking, they are those who attempt to rob our children of joy, peace, vitality, and authentic love; they are the voices that contradict the good news of the Gospel.

We, as fathers, having charitable authority over our families, are called to transmit the liberating truth of the Gospel to our children in order that they may have life to the full. Herod, or Satan, attempts to rob our children of the life of Christ by rivaling our authority, our voice, our ability to lead. He attempts to delegitimize us and intimidate us, hoping to diminish our power to lead.

Remember that if the thief desires to plunder a house, he must first bind the strong man. To bind the human father, the evil one uses intimidation to bully him into believing that he is not capable of being the spiritual leader of his family.

Second, the enemy uses distractions, particularly a man's occupation and hobbies, in order to steal a father's attention from his children.

Third, the devil and his minions use temptations to keep the human father from effectively transmitting God's grace to his children. If the evil one is successful, the human father loses his identity and becomes incapable of leading his family to their destiny. He becomes trapped in boyhood and succumbs to the ultimate desolation of isolation, living a life of loneliness—a life that lacks true, authentic communion with his wife and children.

In other words, the enemy will strive to diminish your effectiveness as a leader by keeping you from prayer and from leading your family in prayer (intimidation), from placing your occupation at the service of your vocation (distraction), and from becoming a man of sacrifice and secrecy, who builds his family into an icon of the Trinity (temptation).

We will discuss each of these three areas individually. But before we do, let's examine these three tactics of the devil and how they apply to our children in a general sense.

Our Children's Enemies:
The World, the Flesh, and the Devil

Just as the enemy attempts to keep us from discovering our identity, particularly as fathers and men who have been divinely endowed with the authority to lead our families, the evil one also attempts to rob our children of their identity, lest they become who God created them to be, and become manifestations of His glory.

The enemy appeals to our children in the three ways that he appeals to us: intimidation, distraction, and temptation. Or, as St. John explains, the three ways that the enemy besets us are the flesh, the world, and the devil.

The evil one tempts our children with the flesh. The enemy seduces them with disordered fleshly appetites that our children consume with their eyes, their ears, their mouths, and sometimes with their entire bodies. We subconsciously sense that there is something deeply troubling about our culture, that our children are under attack, and that our families are very vulnerable to the wiles of the wicked one.

Due to the social-techno revolution, our kids speak an altogether foreign language. As children, many of us thought that our parents were out of touch, that they simply didn't "get it." Today's kids live in a culture saturated with screen names and provocative selfies—a virtual world that speaks in a virtual language that most parents simply cannot relate to, see, or detect. Our children are consumed with social media, hook-up apps, porn websites, violent video games, and unrestricted streaming videos online.

The largest group of porn users are teens between the ages of twelve and seventeen.[3] They live (or die) on a steady diet of daily porn. Studies are now revealing that by the age of nineteen many young men experience erectile dysfunction as a result of porn use, and as they age, they prefer pornography over a real person.

Social technology is the new normal context in which to meet another. Young people in their twenties would now rather hook up via social media apps than court or date someone, because the challenge to have a meaningful conversation and actually socialize normally is too intense.

The generational divide between us and our children is alarming, diabolical, and intentional. The family has been redefined, and what was once known as the traditional family—father, mother, and children—is often viewed by young people as a fairy-tale ideal. Young people understand broken marriages, divorce, single parenting, children living with parents with multiple partners, and same-sex parents as the new norm. Meanwhile, the "good dads" are doing their best to raise good kids by having their children attend Catholic or parochial or private schools, believing that this type of education should "do the trick" and make their children upstanding, successful, moral citizens. Unfortunately, the stats tell a different story: some 80 percent of those who leave the Catholic Church do so before age twenty-three.[4] The satanic tsunami is rolling in and most of the world is hanging around to take pictures. Who can stop the black tide of death from sweeping away our families?

The evil one intimidates our children with the world. Our children want to belong, to "fit in," to be accepted, and if they do not have a strong sense of belonging at home, they will look for belonging elsewhere. Our children are constantly pressured to deny their true selves and become absorbed in trends, fads, and unnecessary needs.

Our youth are intimidated into believing that they have no inherent value and consequently allow their peers to determine their value. If our children do not sense their value at home they will sell themselves out, devaluing themselves to obtain a false sense of being valued.

Ultimately, the peer pressure, or world pressure of intimidation, and the temptation to feed their disordered fleshly appetites lead our children to succumb to the enemy's third tactic—rebellion, the mark of the devil.

The devil is the poster child of rebellion and defiance. "For rebellion is as the sin of divination, and stubbornness is as iniquity and idolatry [demon worship]" (1 Sam. 15:23). A child's rebellious behavior can cause a father to have a profound sense of helplessness, a sense of utter failure and even hopelessness.

Would you consume water that is transferred from the municipal water facility to your faucet if it were laced with arsenic? Would you continue to purchase meat from the local grocery store if it were tainted with botulism? I hope not. Why, then, do we allow our children to be poisoned with the temptation, intimidations, and distractions offered via television, the Internet, radio, and social media? Are we afraid of hurting their feelings by implementing restrictions that will actually set them free?

This is a tremendous challenge for a father. As St. John Paul II said, "There is no love without truth, and no truth without love."[5] Pope Benedict XVI added, "Love without truth is sentimentalism and truth without love is cold and insensitive."[6] It is vital that we fathers challenge ourselves to determine ways to allow our children to live in the world without being consumed by it. Television, radio, digital media, social media usage, and all the rest, if not properly managed, can rob a father of his divinely given authority and lead his children to become selfish and rebellious. It is imperative that we fathers take measures to reclaim our authority.

Like my friend Scott, every man, deep in the recesses of his soul, desires to be courageous enough to sacrifice himself for the sake of his children. A shepherd, at the end of a long day of pasturing his flock, would lead his sheep into the sheepfold. Then he would lay down at the opening, or gate area, to ensure that if a predator tried to enter the fold to devour the sheep, it would have to do so over his dead body.

As fathers, we are called as shepherds of our household to stand guard and defend our children from harmful influences. This could mean that we stop having certain friends over, or stop allowing the kids to have certain friends over, or start spending more time at home with the family.

It could mean that we watch less television, or only the kind of programming that won't damage our children's souls (or our own). It could mean that we discontinue the cable service and have only one television located in a frequently trafficked room rather than having one television in each of the kids' rooms.

Perhaps, if we allow our children to have mobile devices, we have the children leave them with us before trekking off to the bedroom to retire for the evening. Perhaps we install filtration software such as Covenant Eyes on all our computers and mobile devices. Perhaps we begin having our children's friends over to our house so that we know who they are spending time with.

Regardless, it is vital that we engage and embrace our duty to protect our family. Because if we don't, who will? It is time to reclaim our divinely given duty to exercise charitable authority over our family. If no one will lead, there will be none to follow.

To become great leaders we need to become great followers ourselves. To lead our children to Christ we need to be led by Christ. In other words, I cannot give what I do not have. My children will follow me, regardless of whom I follow. Considering this, it is best to follow Christ, because He is the person to whom we want to lead them.

SECRET 4

EMBRACE THE SILENCE

The Voice

Salmon are defined as being anadromous, that is, they are fish that swim upstream. Annually, thousands upon thousands of salmon, after living in the ocean, reaching full maturity, and accumulating full body mass, migrate upstream to return to their place of origin. The human being, like a salmon, is programmed by God to run upward, to return to his Origin.

God creates everything by the power of His Word. God created the universe, the solar systems, seas, stars, the human person—his mind, his heart—by means of His Word. God, through His Word, thought, desired, and spoke you into existence for a particular purpose: to be an expression of His glory to those around you, while also achieving your destiny—full communion and eternal union with God.

But before God sealed you for delivery into this world, He whispered His Word, His Voice, into you. This divine Word is sealed within us. It is hardwired, programmed, into us. The Latin word from which we derive the word vocation is "*vox*," which means "voice." It is this vox of God, this call, that defines your vocation, your identity, and your call to greatness. This vox, this vocation, is programmed into you. It may haunt you, but it will never leave you. This voice within will chase after you, while calling you to chase after it.

It is this voice, this vocation that calls you to run upward, to return to your Origin. Unfortunately, by doing so, like the salmon, which become easy prey during their migration, so also do we land squarely in the evil one's crosshairs. It is precisely in the midst of our vocational path that Satan stands, poised and ready to intimidate us, always striving to instill doubts and feelings of inadequacy and insecurity within us. And there lies the battle, the battle that rages in the heart of man and that will endure until his last breath. His is the battle to trust that he is a son of the Father. As mentioned earlier, to become a great father we must first become a great son who trusts in the greatest Father. The essence of a son is his trust in the Father.

We are like soldiers on the battlefield who have the difficult task of deciphering the real message being transmitted among the false signals. Whose voice, whose message are we receiving—our commander's or our enemy's message? It is imperative that we become capable of sifting through the contradictory messages to discern the voice of our Commander.

The Father Wound

John is one of three brothers whose dad owns a successful auto body shop. His dad expected that all of his sons would take up his trade and spend their adult lives employed in his garage. John, however, had ambitions to attend college and become a teacher. His dad consistently mocked him, referring to him as a "schoolgirl" or a "college idiot." After decades of being a successful, highly effective teacher, the chair of his department, and the winner of numerous teaching awards, he has struggled and fought to shake the nagging sense that he is a failure, that he is not a real man, that he is not the chosen son in whom his father delights.

David was a man's man. The women adored David. Why wouldn't they? He was the stereotypical tall, dark, handsome, big brown-eyed Italian Stallion. I enjoyed being around him, but when standing next to him, I couldn't help feeling like a Munchkin from *The Wizard of Oz*. He would often stop by the office for a visit or for lunch. When he left, my female coworkers (married or not) would literally hang out the second-story office windows to watch him swagger down Main Street to his Ford 4x4.

But David, though dating many, many, many women, could not maintain a single serious relationship. After we became good friends, he confided to me that he was once married, but that he returned home early from a business trip and discovered his wife in bed with his best friend.

He said that the pain, the anguish, the betrayal penetrated him so deeply that it nearly killed him. Because of that horrific event, despite David's handsome, masculine, and attractive qualities, he struggled to believe that he was a real man—a man capable of being vulnerable enough to give himself away to a woman in marriage.

Dan was the victim of his mother's temper and rage. From the earliest years, he was beaten with everything from yardsticks to umbrellas, and locked in his room without food for days on end. He became emasculated. Because of this, from his earliest years he always deferred to women, looking to the female sex for affirmation, a sense of worth and value. Several years after his wedding, Dan's marriage imploded because he had put too great expectations on his wife, expecting her to fulfill his longings and desires. He derived his identity from her attention, but neither she, nor any human being, could provide that type of affirmation. Only God can.

Like John, David, and Dan, we have all been wounded, and the wounds cut deep, causing all sorts of disordered behaviors. These disordered behaviors are defense mechanisms that help cover the wounds. However, by covering our wound, our true self can also become hidden, if not buried.

To survive and hide the wound, the pain, and the fear, we develop coping mechanisms, pseudo selves that hide the person God created us to become.

Every father is called by God to be an expression of His glory, a revelation of God the Father. Satan, however, is determined to intimidate us to ensure that we "cover up" that glory. His tactic is simple. He finds our vulnerability—our weak spot—and wounds us in that area. John became vulnerable by expressing his desire to be a teacher. David became vulnerable by sharing his life with a woman. Dan was vulnerable in his early years of innocence. The enemy stole that innocence by convincing him that if his mother could not be trusted, then it seemed logical that no one can be trusted.

The enemy convinces us that being wounded is our fault. "If you were only more of a man, your wife wouldn't have cheated on you." "If you were a better kid, your mom would have loved you." "If you weren't such a wimp, your dad would have supported you." Consequently, we cover the wound to protect ourselves from being hurt again, but by covering the wound, we also cover up the real person, the revelation of God being manifested through us.

We say to ourselves, "I'm not going to let that happen again. If I do this, or act like this, or dress like that, or if I protect myself from them, then people will like me." Thinking this way, we develop pseudo personalities that hide the true self that God desires us to be in order to express His glory.

Many psychologists identify this wound in men as the "father wound." This means that a man grows up feeling inferior, sensing his inadequacy, and operating from a significant disadvantage because of the limitations, deficiencies, errors, and perhaps neglect and absence of his human father.

At first glance, this appears to make a lot of sense, and gives a man a sense of relief, in that he understands that his deficiencies as a man are not completely his fault—in fact, they are mostly his father's fault.

In some cases, a man's father may have wounded him terribly, causing him to behave in a dysfunctional manner. That presents a dilemma, however: how can we blame our fathers for our dysfunction and not expect our children to blame us for theirs? Is the problem really the father? Is it all his fault?

The father wound entered David by way of his wife and his best friend. He actually had a great relationship with his father. Dan's father wound was delivered by his mother. Sure, Dan's dad could have been present more to defend him, but it was the mother who dealt the blow. The point is this: the father wound can be transmitted by a father, a mother, an uncle, a sibling, or a friend. The human father is not always the source of the "father wound."

What, then, is the father wound exactly?

Although the father wound does not necessarily indicate that a man has been wounded by his father, in all cases there is another "father" whose malice is the reason for the existence of the wound.

The Word and the Wound

My friend Greg likes to describe things with vivid, picturesque imagery in order to drive home a point. Case in point: he will often describe an attractive idea that contains "mostly" truth, but a little nontruth, as having "a little poop in the brownie." "Oh, the brownies are soooooo good," he would say sarcastically, "even if there is a little poop in them." Nobody likes poop in their brownies, and no one likes being duped into believing an attractive truth, only to discover later that it is a lie.

Lingering in the back of many men's minds is the idea that God is after us, out to get us, and if we make one false move, either to the left or to the right, we're gone. Others believe that it is not that God is as much against them as that he is simply not for them; He is absent, uncaring, remote.

We often think something like this: God is perfect. I am a sinner. He is the judge, and I am guilty. This guilt tends to haunt us, and secretly accuse us. In fact, at a very subconscious level, we may believe that because of this guilt, this sin, God is not really for us.

Often, there exists within the shadows of our heart this idea that God is actually out to make our lives miserable. Sometimes the idea manifests itself as a subtle feeling of guilt for experiencing pleasure, or perhaps a belief that God doesn't want us to succeed, or perhaps we have caught the idea that we should not be too happy, lest we forget that we are scum of the earth sinners who deserve to be blown off the face of the globe into eternal oblivion.

But at least when we are feeling like this, we can be thankful and trust that God the Father sacrificed His Son so that we don't have to experience the divine wrath. Right?

Wrong.

This is the attractive "truth" that we have not been taught as much as we have caught. This is a big fat, demonic lie. This is the poop in the brownie.

We may not have been taught the idea that God the Father sacrificed His Son, but we have caught this idea, and it has slithered its way into our subconscious. And while the proposal appears to have the same promise, hope, and relief as blaming my own father for all my disorders, it is simply poop in the brownie. Perhaps the reason so many men believe that God is out to get them is because they believe, somewhere in their mind, that God killed His own Son, and if He is willing to kill His own Son, what is stopping Him from killing us?

God the Father, however, did not kill His Son. We did. Our sins cost him His life. God desires to heal our woundedness. And He accomplishes this by becoming the most wounded—the crucified Son. God became man to offer Himself for us that by dying as a man, we men might live for God. It was not God who killed the Son, but rather the evil one, through men, who killed the Son. God the Son freely offered Himself to God the Father, on behalf of men, so that men would be empowered by His grace to freely offer themselves to God.

Many of us operate from a disadvantage. Many of us have inherited a type of spiritual blindness, and this condition is often the result of the father wound. But what is the father wound?

In the beginning, Adam and Eve, our first parents, lived in harmonious communion with God. God gave them dominion over and access to all things, with the exception of the fruit of the tree of the knowledge of good and evil. From this we learn that God the Father is generous and desires for us to have all that He has. But in order to give us the choice to freely receive that divine generosity, He gave us an option: to love God as He loves us, or to love ourselves above God.

God did not give us the tree of knowledge of good and evil as a dirty trick, but rather as a means of giving us the freedom to prove our love. Without freedom to choose, God would be coercing us into loving Him. But God is a "gentleman" in that He does not force us to do anything, just as He did not force His Son to offer His life. God simply gives us the freedom to choose to love.

But we voted, and we lost the election. We chose selfishness instead of selflessness. We chose slavery to sin, instead of freedom to love; we chose to make ourselves god rather than allow God to make us like Him. The serpent tempted the woman, saying, "You will not die. For God knows that when you eat of it your eyes will be opened, and you will be like God, knowing good and evil" (Gen. 3:4–5).

It was in that moment that Satan cut deep into the heart of the human person, inflicting the ever-haunting father wound. Satan attempts to convince us, as he did our first parents, that God doesn't want us to succeed, that He is "keeping something from us," and that He is "out to get us." As St. John Paul II said, "Original sin, then, attempts to abolish fatherhood."[1]

Even if your father was an absent, neglectful, even abusive man, the father wound was inflicted by the father of lies through your father. The evil one is constantly attempting to mix the messages that God is transmitting to us. The enemy continually attempts to aggravate the father wound, to reopen it, to ensure that it never heals. Because if it doesn't heal, then he can be assured that we do not become icons of God the Father.

This is precisely the satanic agenda. Interestingly enough, it is God's agenda that we "shall be like him" (1 John 3:2). Recall that our understanding of the identity of God determines our identity, and our identity determines not only our destiny but has tremendous influence and impact upon our family's destiny.

To defeat the evil one and his minions, we must strive to overcome the father wound and the sense of insecurity, inadequacy, doubt, mistrust, and discouragement that it causes. We need the Word to heal the wound. In order to overcome the devil's tactic of intimidation, we need to embrace silence and train ourselves to hear the vox.

Speaking God's Language: Silence

To know who we are—to know God's mission, vision, and plan for our lives—we must know God. To know God, we must speak His language, and to paraphrase St. John of the Cross, God's first language is silence.[2]

It is in silence that God speaks, and without sound that His voice is heard. As the psalmist says of God, "Sacrifice and offering you do not desire; but you have given me an open ear" (Ps. 40:6).

Perhaps you've heard this saying: We have two ears and one mouth, therefore we should listen twice as much as we talk. Or maybe you've heard that when one is in the presence of someone more intelligent and knowledgeable than ourselves, we should listen. These ideas can be applied to our relationship with God. When with God, we should listen more than talk.

This message is confirmed by the fact that Christ's public ministry began and ended with miracles pertaining to the act of listening. At the wedding of Cana, where Christ performed His first miracle by transforming water into wine, Mary told the servants, "Do whatever he tells you" (John 2:5). In other words, listen. The last miracle of Christ's public ministry occurred after Peter cut off the ear of Malchus, the high priest's slave. Jesus restores Malchus' ear.

The message is clear: God desires to restore our spiritual hearing. God is calling men to open their ears and not simply hear, but actively and intently listen.

Silence and Space

From the moment I was born into this world, I was busy. I was born to move, and kept moving. The first eight years of my life were one single, running, blur of motion, until Memorial Day of that eighth year. My brother and our friend Billy and I were playing home run derby in our backyard.

Dad had a chain-link fence built, which caged us boys in the backyard, and he also built a picket fence around the front yard, which sat next to a high-traffic, four-lane street. Fifty-third Street was an efficient way to travel from the east side to the west side of town without being stopped by too many lights, and because of that, drivers took advantage of the open road, often moving well beyond the 35-mile-per-hour speed limit.

Mom was adamant that we "keep the ball in the yard" and "absolutely, under no circumstances, go in the street." Like most Memorial Days, at least the ones I have experienced, it began to rain. I had just slugged a "home run" across the two yards, into, and across Fifty-third Street. Billy and my brother decided to go indoors while I chased after the ball. I looked both ways and didn't see or hear any oncoming vehicles, but since we lived at the bottom of a crest in the road, it was difficult for this little eight-year-old to be certain that the road was clear.

I was only a couple of steps into the road when a vehicle operated by a drunk driver, moving well beyond the speed limit, darted over the rise in the street and struck me, punting me to the side of the road. The collision was so intense that the print of my denim jacket was etched into the car's fender. Eight years of constant motion was suddenly stopped in its tracks.

Several moments after returning to consciousness, not understanding where I was, I eventually realized that I was being carried securely in a man's arms. As my world jostled up and down, I heard something—something I had never heard before that day. As he ran, carrying my limp body back to our house, I heard my dad's panicked, heavy breathing, and in his breathing I sensed a pained concern for me.

My father picked up my nearly lifeless body from the side of the road, brought me to safety and the medics, and saved my life. It was in my utter helplessness that my father carried me, and while he carried me I could hear his love for me.

We too, in a certain sense, are helpless. We need the Father to carry us and bring us and our families to safety. However, this demands that we recognize our dependency upon the Father and our need to hear His voice, His love for us.

Many of us move at an almost frantic pace. We are busy. But as it has been said, B.U.S.Y. is an acronym for "burdened under Satan's yoke." It is difficult to pause and carve out time and space to hear the Father's voice, but I suspect that if we did stop and listen, we would hear something like the sound I heard that eighth Memorial Day—the sound of a Father who loves us and is deeply concerned about our lives, and who desires that we live.

It is vital that we stop our hurried lives daily, if not several times a day, to receive the breath of the Father—the Holy Spirit—into our hearts. Our future and our children's future depend to a great extent upon our willingness to do this. To become like the Father we must know the Father. We cannot give to our wives and our children what we do not possess. We can only give Christ's presence if we have Christ's presence within us.

God always generously gives us His presence, but in order to make room for that generous presence, we must carve out time and space for God, and train ourselves to listen attentively to the Word of the Father.

Besides the temptations to feed our lusts and caress our ego, dedicating time and space to God is perhaps among the greatest challenges facing men. But by doing so, we will be more capable of dismissing Satan's voice of intimidation, and able to listen to and trust in a God who loves us and has claimed us as His own.

Making Space

During Israel's wanderings in the desert, Moses erected what was called a tent of meeting, outside the Israelite camp, where individuals could go for the purpose of seeking consultation with God. From this account, we learn several things: First, Moses erected a place dedicated specifically to meeting with God. Second, this place of meeting was outside the camp, that is, it was away from the place where the Israelites' daily activities took place. Third, God met with Moses and others, offering consolation and guidance.

To be successful fathers, we need to hear the voice of the Father, and to do this, we need to establish our own tent of meeting—a place of prayer outside the camp of daily life. In other words, we ought to find or create a space dedicated exclusively to God—away from the electronics,

the projects and paperwork, and the messes of daily life—
and set aside time to meet with God in this space.

Your place of meeting could be your attic, an empty
room, or the adoration chapel down the street. But it
should be close and accessible. By separating the space
from life's daily clutter, you will remove distractions. It
is difficult enough to pray without being distracted in a
place dedicated exclusively to God, let alone while in your
office, or worse, amidst the piles of toys or dirty laundry.

Making Time

Besides space, we need to set aside quality time for God.
One of the secrets to a rich prayer life is to arise before the
rest of the family. Remember that it was Mary Magdalene
who rose before the dawn on Resurrection Sunday to anoint
the body of Jesus, and it was also Mary who was the first
to see the resurrected Christ.

It is ideal if a father meets with the Lord morning, noon,
and at night, and builds his day around God, rather than
God around his day.

One of the keys to a successful prayer life is consistency.
Assign particular times of day for your time with God
and protect them zealously. I've heard of some men who
consider those times so sacred that no appointments or
meetings can be scheduled during their prayer times.

If prayer times are not set at certain times of the day, they
will undoubtedly be brushed aside to make room for the
latest fire or urgent request. We all have certain things we
guard jealously: our favorite television show, our favorite
NFL team's game time, date night with our wife, cigar
night with the guys—but there is nothing as important as
your prayer life, and it should be protected as seriously.

The degree to which you protect your prayer life will be the degree to which you protect your family.

The Power of Prayer

Prayer is where we obtain the power to become men of greatness. Several years ago, a computer technician installed a back-up drive and software on my work computer. After approximately a week, I noticed that the drive was not archiving my data properly. I contacted the technician, who ran me through a series of resolutions over the phone. Nothing worked. Finally, he said, "Devin, check to see if the unit is plugged in." To which I responded, "Of course it's plugged in." He insisted, "Devin, just check." Sure enough, it was not plugged in.

The back-up unit was new, in good functioning condition, and perfectly capable of fulfilling the task for which it was created. However, it was not connected to its power source and therefore was useless.

We are like my back-up unit. To be effective fathers it is vital that we are connected to our power source—God—by means of the power cord—prayer. If we are not connected to God by prayer, regardless of how many talents, gifts, and abilities we have, we will be rendered useless in God's plan.

Carving out silence and space for God allows you to be infused with His peace, joy, love, power, strength, resilience, and patience (to mention a few of His gifts). It is your job to transmit these characteristics to your children by your example. We cannot give what we do not have, but we can give what we've been given.

Years ago, the advertising agency for which I worked brought in a seasoned marketing expert from Disneyland who, during one of his seminars, explained how Disneyland plays certain types of music to keep consumers motivated and moving from one exhibit, ride, or game to another. The music sets the rhythm and the pace to which their patrons marched. This is the evil one's tactic: he plays the song "get it done," "run from this engagement to that one," "keep going," "be productive," "stay tuned in," to ensure that we march to his beat and never stop to hear the voice of God —the voice that calls you to your mission of greatness.

In his cleverly insightful *Screwtape Letters*, C. S. Lewis exposes the evil one's agenda. Screwtape, an archdemon, writes a letter to his demon nephew, Wormwood:

> Music and silence—how I detest them both! How thankful we should be that ever since our Father [the devil] entered Hell . . . no square inch of infernal space and no moment of infernal time has been surrendered to either of those abominable forces, but all has been occupied by Noise—Noise, the grand dynamism, the audible expression of all that is exultant, ruthless, and virile . . . We will make the whole universe a noise in the end. We have already made great strides in this direction as regards the Earth.[3]

One of the most difficult things for a hardworking, diligent man to do is to stop the busyness, shut off the radio, bury the mobile phone, and snuff out the kingdom of noise. By calming the chaos, silencing the noise, and entering into our sacred space and the silence that God offers, we can receive the Father's guidance.

The Offering

I can be a bit sentimental. I remember, as a kid, watching *The Little Drummer Boy* and being struck by the message that he had no gift to bring but himself and his drum. He played his best for the baby in the manger, and out of all the people who brought Him gifts, the little drummer boy was the one who was rewarded with the Babe smiling at him.

As adults we tend to complicate things. We develop strategies, flow charts, and mechanisms all at the service of making things more efficient. It's like that with prayer. We tend to create all sorts of formulas, techniques, and positions, when God is interested in one thing: me and my drum. That is, the drumbeat of my heart.

Recall that God the Father did not coerce His Son to sacrifice Himself on behalf of men. The Father did not kill or sacrifice Jesus. Together, they offered themselves to the other. God will not take from us what we do not give. God will not force us into offering ourselves to Him. He leaves that choice to us.

Prayer is an offering of oneself to God—it's that simple. And it's that difficult.

The idea of praying can often intimidate a man, make him feel as though he is wasting his time, or that he is not holy enough to "hear" God's voice. However, praying is simply presenting oneself, one's experiences, with trust in the Lord that He will infuse His presence into us and our experiences.

We most likely will not hear God's audible voice. But that's okay. Our soul is primary to our body and our spirit gives form to the body. This means that God speaks first and foremost to our souls, and this infusion of His Word will give form to our lives. God will often speak to our spirit in ways that the body cannot comprehend, but nevertheless we will, over time, experience growth in wisdom and charity and notice that we are being guided upon a truly divine path.

Prayer is much like a blood transfusion. Consider that when you have a blood transfusion you do nothing more than remain still and allow the old blood to be replaced by new blood. You don't have to understand the process for it to be effective. Prayer is like that. Often, all we need to do in order for prayer to be effective is simply to sit still and remain in the presence of God and allow Him to infuse us with His divine life.

If a man presents himself to God, God will give His presence to that man. Our Lord promised, "and him who comes to me I will not cast out" (John 6:37).

To present oneself to God mandates that we present our real self, with all of our sins, shortcomings, inadequacies, weaknesses, deficiencies, and errors, while also acknowledging and thanking God for the gifts, abilities, and talents that He has afforded us—precisely those gifts that appear to be uniquely different from the gifts of those around us. St. Francis de Sales said that this form of prayer defeats pride, because it helps us acknowledge that these unique gifts are from God and not ourselves.

A Father's Interior Life
Gives His Family Life Form

Sometimes it can be difficult to assess ourselves and determine the bad and the good, the failings and successes, our sins and our gifts. We need something that will help launch us into conversation with God, a springboard that will allow us to dive into the mystery of God, while also understanding the mystery that we are.

Our Lord Jesus, in the Sermon on the Mount, alluded to a simple, three-step, effective way for fathers to pray: "Or what man of you, if his son asks him for bread, will give him a stone? Or if he asks for a fish, will give him a serpent? If you then, who are evil, know how to give good gifts to your children, how much more will your Father

who is in heaven give good things to those who ask him!"
(Matt. 7:9–11).

First, notice that Jesus invites each of us to come to our
place of prayer with something—namely ourselves and
our fatherly experiences. We bring our experiences as a
father to our place of prayer, present them to the Father
and meditate upon them, attempting to discover what God
desires to disclose to us by means of those experiences.

Second, by meditating upon these experiences we begin
to compare our sentiments for our children to God the
Father's love for us. When Jesus asks, "What man of you,
if his son asks him for bread, will give him a stone. . ," He
is inviting fathers to compare human fatherhood to God's
fatherhood. We who are "evil" want good gifts for our
children, yet how much more does the Father care for us
and our children? These experiences—which reveal our
love, hopes, and desires for our children—if meditated
upon, afford us a window into the Father's love for us
and our children. The point is that if we, being made in
the image and likeness of God, desire good things for our
children, how much more does our Father in heaven desire
that which is truly best for us?

Which leads us to the third step: we realize by means
of the comparison that God loves us and desires so much
more for us than we can imagine.

To review: First, we bring our experiences of fatherhood
to prayer. Second, we compare our feelings, reactions, and
responses as a father to God and His love for us. And
third, by means of this comparison, we realize that God
has chosen us and takes delight in us as His own sons.

For example, you may recall while praying that your
seven-year-old son incessantly followed you around the
house, talking nonstop, persistently asking you to play with
him. Meditating upon this, you might discover that your

son simply admires you, desires your attention, and wants to be an important part of your life. By comparing your fatherhood to God's fatherhood, you may realize that you are not quite perfect. Your son was annoying you, so you did not respond properly. Does God the Father treat you this way? God says, "I am with you always, to the close of the age" (Matt. 28:20). Though father and mother will forsake you, He will never forsake you (Ps. 27:10). From this you understand the perfect love of the Father and ask God to help you to become like Him, to change and become a better dad. When your prayer has ended you leave with that desire in mind.

Several years ago, my oldest daughter, at the age of fourteen, suddenly began losing her hair and was balding rapidly. At the onset, I thought her condition was in my imagination. However, she also began to lose a significant amount of weight.

As you can imagine, I became overwhelmed with fear, and concerned that she could be dying. I felt helpless. As I prayed about her situation, I began to consider how, if I could, I would be willing to suffer in her place. I would be willing to go bald, lose weight, become sick, just to ensure that she would live. By meditating upon these thoughts and comparing them to God's fatherhood, I was reminded that God actually did take my place, and took the sickness of my sin and suffering upon Himself to ensure that I have life—life to the full.

Our interior life gives our exterior life form. Our private prayers will manifest publicly the presence of the Lord, who lives within us. A father who prays privately will eventually lead his family in prayer. And as Fr. Peyton said, "A family that prays together stays together."

It is our duty as fathers to protect our family by leading them in prayer so that they can learn how to have a relationship with Jesus and His Father. If you don't teach them, who will? We ought to lead them to Holy Mass, lead prayer at meals or evening prayer, even if it is only a decade of the rosary, or read the Gospel of the day. Our interior life gives our family life form.

St. Joseph: A Man of Prayer

Recall that we first encounter St. Joseph during a tremendous vocational crisis. Satan, the intimidator, was standing in Joseph's vocational path, attempting to instill doubt into Joseph's heart, tempting him to believe that he should withdraw from his vocation. How did Joseph respond to the dilemma? He retreated into silence and listened. In fact, not a single spoken word of Joseph's is recorded. This should give us strong, silent types some encouragement. Joseph's prayer was so intense that he prayed about the dilemma even while he slept.

"But *as he considered this*, behold, an angel of the Lord appeared to him in a dream, saying, 'Joseph, son of David, do not fear to take Mary your wife, for that which is conceived in her is of the Holy Spirit'" (Matt. 1:20, emphasis added).

We must not overlook this point. Joseph did not sleep through his crisis. Scripture says, "as he considered this," meaning that he was considering his crisis when the angel appeared in a dream. Nor did Joseph have it easy because an angel transmitted divine messages to him.

Rather, Joseph entered the silence and listened so profoundly that he was capable of hearing God's message—the vox, God's voice within him—calling him to his vocational path to greatness, awakening him to his identity and mission.

If we want direction for our lives, if we want to return to our origin, if we want to know our identity and destiny, we must be determined to carve out time and space for God and listen. In fact, if we want our children to listen to us, their fathers, we children must be willing to listen to the Father.

Notice that it was during Joseph's crisis that he turned to God, waiting for the Lord to direct him, and received his mission to be the husband of the Mother of God and the father of God the Son. You and I will encounter multiple crises throughout our lifetimes, and these crises, if embraced and presented to the Lord, will allow us to discover the real man inside. But the success of this endeavor is contingent on listening to the Lord and responding to His still, small voice.

SECRET 5

WORK FOR GOD

Motives Matter

Motives matter. Take for instance, a four-year-old boy who climbs over the arm of the chair and snuggles into his mother's lap, gazes tenderly into her eyes, and says, "Mom, you're the prettiest woman in the whole wide world." His mom's eyes light up with life, her heart melts as she gives him a gentle squeeze. Not more than a second later, the boy asks, "Mom, can I have a piece of candy?" Suddenly, the compliment that caused her soul to soar has been revealed for what it truly was—a form of manipulation.

On one occasion, my youngest daughter, two at the time, confessed to her mother and me that she wanted to die. We were crushed. Already, at two years of age, my daughter was having a midlife crisis. When her mom asked her why, she responded, "Because I want to go to heaven and be with Jesus."

Motives matter.

Many actions, from an external viewpoint, appear to have the same character, but it is the interior motivation behind the action that gives the action meaning. God Himself, speaking to the prophet Samuel, said something very similar: "For the LORD sees not as man sees; man looks on the outward appearance, but the LORD looks on the heart" (1 Sam. 16:7).

This truth can be applied to our work. Why do we work? What is the true motive behind fulfilling our work? Some men simply work to receive a wage—that's it, nothing more. Others work because it gives them a sense of fulfillment, dignity, and value. Others work because they sense that they have a mission to place their gifts and talents at the service of the people around them. Some men work because they enjoy it. There are elements of truth in each of these motives, and yet there exists a deeper, more fundamental meaning to a father's work.

Years ago, while on a retreat at a monastery, I was eating alone in the refectory when a young priest approached me, introduced himself, and eventually asked, "What do you do?" I responded, "I am a father." Visibly perplexed and somewhat surprised, he replied, "Oh . . . You're a priest?" I realized that I needed to clarify my statement and explain that I wasn't a priest. I told him, "No, I'm a dad."

Afterward, I reflected on that conversation and my response to the young priest, and discovered that over the years my thinking had changed. Traditionally, when asked what I do, I'd describe my occupation; but that day, I described my vocation—my identity. My identity is not based upon what I do for a living, but for whom I am living. What I do is different than what I am. At work— whether I like it or not—I am replaceable. At home—as a husband and father, despite what the world tells me—I am irreplaceable. My identity, my greatness, is not rooted fundamentally in my occupation, but rather, it is derived from my vocation.

This truth indicates that my God-given talents are at the service of providing for my family in order that they may be protected, fed, and taught the meaning of life. As men, we have multiple, ongoing responsibilities, most of which belong to one of three categories: God, family, and work. One of the keys to becoming an effective, engaged, and successful father is integrating these three areas of responsibility.

Work and Family: The Tension

In the beginning, at the very onset of creation, God gave us two fundamental commands: raise families and work for our families. "And God blessed them, and God said to them, 'Be fruitful and multiply, and fill the earth and subdue it'" (Gen. 1:28). In other words, raise families. "The LORD God took the man and put him in the garden of Eden to till it and keep it" (Gen. 2:15). In other words, the Lord ordained man to work for his family. Obviously, these two commands are rich with meaning, but at the basic, fundamental level, they are telling us to fill the earth with families, work at raising families, and raise families by means of work.

If, however, family and work are not united by the one who ordained these commands, these two worlds of responsibilities will bite against one another, causing a father to live in continual tension between his family and his work.

The advent of mobile technology has compounded this tension. At the end of the workday, we leave our place of employment, only to discover that, like a stray cat, work has followed us home. Like Sauron's "One Ring," in Tolkien's epic fantasy, *The Lord of the Rings*, that "rules them" and "binds them," our work calls to us—from our phones and from our computers, in an almost overpowering way—distracting us from our families. Distraction is the tool of the enemy.

Often, before we realize what we are actually doing, we set off to be alone with the "Ring of Power"—our work—and leave behind the very reason why we work—our family. As a friend of mine said, "Work can often become the mistress that steals due attention from our wives and children." We often have difficulty "taming" our work, or turning it off. As an acquaintance used to say, "Work will take as much as you give it."

Recall that the evil one uses three basic tactics in order to keep us from realizing our identity: he uses intimidation to keep us from praying, he uses temptation to keep us self-focused rather than other-focused, and he uses distraction, primarily by means of our work, as a way to use work against our family rather than in support of it.

It was close to dinnertime when I arrived home just after purchasing my first smartphone. Before dinner, I delivered an inspiring, beautifully articulated speech to my family, explaining how "this phone does not rule us, but rather, we rule the phone; I am master of my phone, rather than my phone being master of me." It was simply poetic. It was all about leading by example. We proceeded to pray before eating, and just as we ended prayer and finished making the sign of the cross, my new cell phone rang. I jumped out of the chair, grabbed the phone, and answered it. My children's jaws dropped, as they sat motionless—dumbfounded—staring at me in complete disbelief. The "smartphone" was making me more stupid by the second.

As we are called to have mastery over our smartphones and wireless devices, we dads are called to have dominion over our work, not to allow work to have dominion over our families. Work is the servant of the family; the family is not the servant of work.

The Purpose of Work

A father exercises charitable authority, that is, he is called to lead by loving and to love by leading, by protecting, feeding, and teaching. The purpose of our work is to feed the family, both temporally and spiritually. In fact, Jesus' words provide the definitive statement regarding the purpose of a father's labors: "Do not labor for the food which perishes, but for the food which endures to eternal life" (John 6:27).

Our Lord challenges fathers to understand that the ultimate reason for labor is to labor for the true bread that gives eternal life—Jesus Himself. But how does a father labor for Jesus? Jesus' words again give us insight: "Whoever receives this child in my name receives me, and whoever receives me receives him who sent me; for he who is least among you all is the one who is great" (Luke 9:48).

In other words, by receiving a child, that is, by spiritually adopting our children, we receive Christ in that child, but not only Christ, but also the Father with Christ. We labor for Christ in our children, just as Joseph labored for God by laboring for God's Son.

The ultimate purpose of work is to labor for Jesus in our children, with the purpose of further developing Christ in our children. In other words, work is fund-raising for our ministry—our families.

Noticed by Men or Known by God

So why do so many of us spend countless hours at work —even though work tortures us—at the expense of the family? Often, when a father experiences the common, mundane, and often apparently unrewarding character of fatherhood and family life, he is tempted to view work as a viable vehicle for validation—a means to obtain the

affirmation, honor, acclaim, and recognition that he feels
he is not receiving at home.

Work understood in this way becomes an end in itself, a
tool used to serve man's ego, and can become the archenemy
of our children, usurping the attention that they desperately
need. We often justify our actions, believing that we are
giving our children everything that they need: shelter,
clothing, food, education, and spending money. But in the
end, one of the greatest things that they truly desire, need,
and sorely miss is their father's attention and love.

The enemy uses work as a distraction, a way to take
our focus and attention off of what really matters—of *who*
really matters. It is easy to be duped into believing that our
endless hours at work allow our children to live, when, in
reality, those hours at work could be stealing their life.

My wife related a news story describing a horrific inci-
dent concerning a new father whose wife normally dropped
their newborn baby off at the day-care facility on her way
to work. On this occasion, however, the mother was unable
to fulfill the duty, and so the task fell to the father. Consumed, as we all are, with work, the day's agenda, meetings, responsibilities, deadlines, and endless to-do lists, instead of driving to the day-care facility, the father drove
to work. Later, during that hot, summer's day, the father
realized his mistake and frantically returned to his car only
to discover that his baby was dead.

The account is awful, morbid, and incredibly painful
to recount, but what is almost as horrific is the reality
that I have the potential to do the very same thing. I am
constantly being distracted by my obligations to my clients,
by project deadlines, and by management of subcontractors.
Sometimes, my wife and children will speak directly to me
—in front of my very face—and I am internally located
in front of my computer, putting the finishing touches on

my latest project, or editing the final sentence of an e-mail. The evil one uses work to distract us from those for whom we are working.

In fact, by allowing work to distract me, as I do so often, I steal not only precious time away from my children, but also the very life that I would have transmitted to them during those fleeting hours.

Consider, for instance, my writing this book. Writing a book on fatherhood, its glory, power, vitality, and necessity, is a good thing. But I become a hypocrite when *writing* about being a father proves to be an obstacle to my truly *being* a father. It isn't logical to write about the need for fathers when I leave my family in need.

It can be difficult to determine whether I am stealing time away from my family. It is during moments such as these that I need to evaluate my motives. Why am I doing this? What is the purpose of this work? Is it to glorify God, or to glorify myself? Is it to serve myself or serve others? Sometimes these questions can be difficult to answer. That is why we need silence and space to allow God to speak to our souls, to guide us and reveal our true motives.

I can make the argument that this chapter could, potentially, reorient men toward their vocation and, therefore, I am serving them and helping them serve their families. But is this endeavor my primary vocation? Should this work have top priority over my vocation? Most likely not. Perhaps this is why so many good-hearted, goodwilled endeavors accomplished in the name of Christ fail to truly assist in transforming hearts—because they undermine the very truth that they are communicating. This is defined as hypocrisy, which, at its core, is orienting one's life toward being noticed, respected, and affirmed by men, rather than choosing to be known by God.

The enemy appeals to our woundedness, our lack of trust
in the Father, and therefore distracts us, luring us into that
temptation to be noticed by others rather than to be known
by God. The enemy convinces us to be exteriorly active,
seen by others, deriving value from what others think of
us, rather than what God knows of us.

This is a diabolical trap.

Why? Because human respect is shifting sand upon
which no man should build his house—his domestic church.
By living for human respect, a man tends to shift his behavior and shape his personality in order to maintain his
following, keep his fans, and grow his number of friends.
When he loses his following, and falls out of grace with
his friends, he then adapts his personality, his behaviors,
and his appearance in order to please them and win them
over. However, each time that a man shifts his behaviors,
changes his appearance, and adapts his personality with
the purpose of gaining human respect, he moves further
from his true identity. If he continues on such a path, his
false identity will be incapable of leading him toward his
destiny—which ultimately means that he will be unable
to lead his family toward its destiny.

By doing our work to be noticed by men, even if we
fulfill the purpose of providing food for the family, our
motives are flawed. Our families can intuit the difference
between a father who is motivated by his family and a
father who is motivated at the expense of his family.

Deep within us, God has planted an authentic desire for
respect, honor, and glory. These God-given desires, at their
core, are very good. God has given us these desires for the
purpose of glorifying Him, and by glorifying Him we will
be glorified by Him. It is not for us, however, to play God
and determine our own glory, but rather to leave that job
to Him.

Sometimes, however, this authentic desire can become inverted, self-seeking, mutated into a longing to be noticed by men rather than being known by God.

When we live for the respect of men, we risk losing our vocational compass, our very identity—who we are, not what we do. By living for the respect of men, we become a wave tossed about in the ocean, a reed swaying in the wind; we accommodate our personalities to what people think of us, or what we want people to believe about us. This is a perpetually moving target, which runs its course at Mach speed at the approximate distance of the planet Pluto. It cannot be hit. Shooting at this target is more than a misfire—it is a backfire that causes the loss of one's true identity.

When we do not become the person that we are created to be, not only we lose, but our families lose. They lose the presence and glory of God, the very unique presence that God desires us to transmit to them by means of our fatherhood.

As one priest said so eloquently, "Do not become a streetlamp, only to have your house go dark." And another priest advised, "You will become a saint by means of your vocation, not outside of it."

Doing Your Best and Letting God Do the Rest

During the period when I was employed at a local advertising agency, I would, on occasion, work 48-hour marathon shifts without returning home to visit my family. Our creative team was the recipient of many awards, and in the branding world we were revered as being among the most talented. Awards are good, in that they recognize someone for their ingenuity, giftedness, and diligence. I, however, began to crave the awards, working extreme hours for the purpose of taking home the trophy, or to win with the boss —only to be the loser at home.

During that time, I stumbled upon an award-winning ad. The visual was a gray-toned, nostalgic photograph of a four- to five-year-old son, roaring with laughter while sitting upon his dad's shoulders, with arms outstretched pretending to fly. The dad was also smiling from ear to ear. The headline read something like this: "In the end, no dad ever says 'I wish I'd spent more time at the office.'"

Time stood still. I can still remember the cubicle I was located in, the position of my chair, the feeling of disappointment in myself—while also sensing a strange new hope that there was another way, a better way. I wish that I had a door to that office. I would have shut it tight, locked it, and cried my eyes out for the many moments that I missed playing with the kiddos.

As odd as it may sound, that secular ad had a profound effect on my future behavior. I went cold turkey, and began leaving work on time in order to ensure that I would be home for dinner with the family. Nearly twenty years later, I can testify that that decision was one of the most beneficial things I have ever done.

Just to be clear: this does not mean that we accomplish our work in a halfhearted, unprofessional manner. What it does mean is that we don't try to impress the boss at work, but rather the Boss in heaven. We simply do our best, and let God do the rest. We are to use the time that is allocated to work with the purpose of doing everything to the fullness of our capacities, to the best of our abilities. But when that time is up, and the "quitting time" alarm sounds, we ought to be courageous enough to release control and turn it over to God. When we "seek first his kingdom and his righteousness, and all these things shall be [ours] as well" (Matt. 6:33).

As the psalmist says, "It is in vain that you rise up early and go late to rest, eating the bread of anxious toil; for he gives to his beloved sleep" (Ps. 127:2).

Putting the Brakes on Work

My family had just returned from a weekend retreat at Grandpa and Grandma's house in the countryside of Trenton, Iowa. Grandpa had purchased a couple of old Schwinn bicycles from a local auction and gave them to my dad, for him to give to my brother and me. I, being eight at the time, and Dustin, my brother, being six, were chomping at the bit, and could hardly wait to "break them in." The only real challenge was that the only other bike I had ever ridden was my Big Wheel.

Shortly after arriving home, we began testing the bikes. Dad had decided to do some yard work along the picket fence that ran alongside the driveway. As I recall, we took the bikes up the road, to the crest of the hill, since it was too difficult to get the bike started on an incline. Momentum and gravity would aid us in setting the bikes in motion. I was the first to push off.

The bike and I began moving downhill at a moderate pace. I was surprised with my own ability to keep it upright and balanced. It took a couple of moments, but I was finally able to set my little feet squarely on the rotating peddles and began peddling. I was riding a bike! I was a natural! As I cruised down the sidewalk, the bike and I were gaining momentum. It was liberating.

It was in that moment, amidst the exhilaration, that I suddenly realized that I did not know how to stop the bike. I was faced with an incredible choice: I could continue speeding forward, full throttle, straight into the high-traffic, four-lane road with which the road I was on intersected, or I could angle the handle bars slightly to the right and aim for the picket fence, by which my dad was now bent over pulling weeds.

There was no choice. I aimed at the fence. By this time, the bike pedals were spinning at such an incredible rate that my feet could not remain upon them. Paralyzed with fear, without screaming, with legs stretched straight away to the right and to the left, I braced myself for what was about to happen next. I crashed full speed into the fence, inches away from my dad, wedging the front wheel between the wooden slats. The bike instantaneously stopped—but I didn't. My body catapulted—was ejected full force—up and over the fence, face-planting in our front yard. My dad went ballistic. "Devin, you could have killed me!" Then noticing my rear end sunny-side up and my mouth eating dirt, he added, "You could have killed yourself! What are you thinking!"

I did my best to explain that I didn't know how to stop.

Sometimes "stopping" can be difficult, but regardless, it is imperative that we find a way to stop. Stopping the work train by simply slamming on the brakes and denying those to whom we owe a service by means of our work is not the way to stop the work addiction.

Stopping the work train does not mean that we stop working, or simply walk away from our obligations. In fact, if we stop working and cease doing our work well, we are doing a disservice to our family, to our employers, to our clients, and to God. However, if we have discovered that our occupation is encroaching upon our vocation, we must find a way to stop.

Working with God

The experience of working to feed our family is just as much about learning to be dependent upon our Father as it is about providing for those who are dependent upon us.

At the wedding of Cana, Jesus commanded the servants, who represent each of us, to take the six stone jars, used for the Jewish rites of purification, and fill them with water (John 2). The servants filled those six extraordinarily heavy clay vessels, each holding twenty to thirty gallons of water, to the brim. That is a lot of weight and a lot of water. The jars could be considered a symbol of the six days of creation, the six days of work, and the wedding (on day seven) a symbol of God's marriage to man. It was on the seventh day of creation that God made a covenant with man, and it was on this seventh day—at the wedding of Cana—that God renewed His marriage with man.

The servants filled the jars to the brim, that is, they accomplished their work to the fullest of their capacity, and yet, regardless of their superior efforts, the water was still just that—water.

But the message doesn't end there. Jesus, seeing that they accomplished their work with excellence, blessed their work by transforming it into wine, which is a symbol of grace.

It is God's desire that there exists a "marriage" of work between God and man. We are to accomplish our work by laboring for Christ in our children, and we accomplish this work to the best of our ability, always acknowledging that it is fund-raising for our ministry. If we work in this way, God will transform our work—our water—into wine —grace—for ourselves, our family, and those around us. Without our water, there is no wine, and without wine, it is nothing more than water. God desires that we collaborate with Him and work for the bread that doesn't perish, the bread that gives life—Himself. In order for our work to be effective, we need to offer it to God and let Him breathe His grace into our efforts.

Work begins with God, is accomplished ultimately for God, should end with God, and can only be transformed into grace by God. But God desires that you and I supply the water.

The Vitality of Work

God is the Creator, and we creatures have been created in His image and likeness, which indicates that we have been created to create. Only God can create *ex nihilo*, that is, from nothing, and yet God ordains that we image Him by creating with what He has created. After the six days of creation, God didn't stop creating. In fact, Jesus on one occasion said that His Father "works to this very day"—a statement that was nearly the cause of His stoning. When we depart from this world and, by God's saving grace, spend our eternity with God and His elect, we will not cease to create. If we did stop creating, we would cease to image God—which is impossible for those who have become like Him.

Last Christmas, I made the decision to take an extended vacation from work—not to travel somewhere exotic, but simply to spend quality time with my family. As I've mentioned, I am a graphic designer by trade, and spend my work hours generating and creating brands, logos, websites, and promotional materials. In other words, my full-time occupation is to be consistently creative. During this particular Christmas break, I wanted to have a break from creating.

What occurred was nothing short of enlightening.

I drove my wife and my children crazy. They could hardly wait until I returned to work. It was no wonder— I was depressed, tired, and grumpy. I felt like a fish out of water, like a stranger, a foreigner in my own domain. I wandered aimlessly from room to room, like a lost puppy, attempting to discover something meaningful to which I could apply myself. It was pathetic.

Why was I so disgruntled? Why did I feel so disoriented? Because we humans are created to create. We are not called to be production machines, but we are called to create in order to be a gift to those around us. I had no creative outlet, no way to be a creative gift to those around me.

We discover our identity and we experience vitality when we create, especially when we create for the sake of the other. This is what our work is supposed to facilitate— being creative and being a gift to the world around us.

Now, even though I was on vacation and taking time off work, I could have developed a hobby that facilitated authentic creativity. Both our work and our hobbies should have this creative quality.

God our Father creates for us and we as fathers are called to experience His life, His creative vitality, precisely by creating for our families and others. So, far from work being an unnecessary evil, it is necessary in aiding us to discover our very identity, which will lead us to our destiny.

St. Joseph the Worker

St. Joseph was a *tekton*, a Greek word meaning that he was not only a carpenter, but also a craftsman, and perhaps an architect of sorts, who used varying types of substrates and materials in his labors. As a father, Joseph labored in a manner that appears to have great similarity to the method of labor we fathers use today. Rather than hunting for food, or working in the fields to obtain a harvest, Joseph most likely labored for wages by erecting buildings, repairing houses, and perhaps crafting furniture and farming tools.

By gathering wages, Joseph gathered food, which afforded the gathering of his family around that food, in an ode of thanksgiving to God. We, as fathers, are to work for wages in order to gather food, and by gathering food, we gather our family around the food, where we give thanksgiving to God the Father.

This indicates that dinnertime is an essential, pivotal event for the family and the father. During dinner, a father leads prayer, gives thanks for the food around which he gathered his family, and, by thanking God in this manner, he is also gathering his family to the Father.

It is during dinnertime that some of the most important conversations with our children occur. However, it's our job to initiate the conversation. The best way to do that is by asking open-ended questions. Not so much, "How was your day?" But more like, "What did you do today?" Not so much, "How was school?" But rather, "What did you learn in school today?" Not so much, "Why are you flunking out of Math?!?!!?" But instead, "Great job on that English paper."

Dinnertime should be a place of safety and affirmation and a refuge for the children and family. The dinner table is not a good place for criticism, sarcasm, or drilling the children about why they are not doing their chores, or why they are struggling at school. Rather, a father should take that time to be encouraging, facilitating conversation about all of life and encouraging laughter and joy. A father should ask questions about his children's lives, their school, their friends, their desires and hopes. He should avoid condemning or handing out to-do lists. Dinnertime is an event of deep communion among members of the family.

We experience this dynamic at Holy Mass. Our Lord Jesus, the New Adam, the new Father of our race, gathers us around His food, His offering, His bread of life—His Body and Blood. He gathers each of us around the Father's "dinner table"—the altar—to ensure that we, by receiving this heavenly bread, can give thanks to God and be gathered to the Father. This means that our dinner table is a symbol of the altar. Our gathering is a symbol of the Church. The human father is a symbol of Christ, who gathers His family to the Father.

From these truths, we can begin to understand the inestimable value of the family dinner, and the familial communion that it creates. The family that eats together . . . well, stays together. We can also begin to understand why Sunday is a sacred day on which no occupational or servile work should be undertaken. Sunday is the definitive sign of the New Covenant and a sign that the human father trusts that his heavenly Father will continue to provide for him.

If our schedules, work, and activities prove to be obstacles to the family gathering at dinnertime, then it may be best to delete or reorganize those events as much as possible. If our work conflicts with keeping the Lord's Day holy, perhaps we need to reassess our motives for work. As with me and my new bicycle, there is a way to stop—even if it is painful.

It is vital that we fathers reclaim our charitable authority, in order to feed our family.

Don't underestimate the power, impact, and effect that family dinners can have on your children's souls. While in college, I fell away from the faith in a big way. I left the Church and began living an immoral—painfully immoral —licentious life, and never considered Christ as real, or even as a source of true, authentic happiness.

After one of my all-night drinking binges, a friend and I went to a local hamburger joint to grab a bite to eat and work off our hangovers.

After ordering my meal, I sat down at a table by myself while my friend placed his order. Just then, a small, delicate, middle-aged woman sat down at a table across from mine. She didn't see me, but I watched her carefully as she bowed her head, closed her eyes, and slowly made the sign of the cross over her body. I couldn't take my eyes off her. In fact, at that moment I believed her to be the most beautiful woman I had seen in years. I was motionless as I watched her pray in silence.

I was internally swept away to my youth. In a momentary flashback, I was sitting in "my chair" at our dinner table, while dad led the prayer before dinner. I was *there*. The peace, the joy of the family, the feeling of being loved, all came crashing back like a tidal wave over my very dry soul. My heart became heavy with longing and my eyes filled with tears. I missed those days, I missed my dad, I missed the security of family and of love. I missed God.

Without taking my eyes off her, I muttered under my breath, "I want that again. I want God."

That moment proved to be the beginning of my return to Christ and His Church—all because of the family dinner.

SECRET 6

SACRIFICE IN SECRET

Identity, Destiny, and Stuff

With seven members, five of whom are children, our family has a tendency to accumulate stuff—a lot of stuff —that we struggle to make room for. The fact that we are limited on closet space makes finding places for everything even more challenging. My family cringes when I cite my oft-repeated mantra, "Places have things and things have places. Everything has its place." Or, speaking of closets and their effect on the entire house, "If the inside is organized, the outside will be organized as well." But what do you do when there simply is not enough space?

My wife and I implemented an effective strategy that helped provide a piece of the solution to the problem of stuff. When the children would spend time outside of the home, for example at Grandma's, we would strategically remove certain toys—hide them in the attic—and wait to see if any of the children noticed that they were missing.

It's cruel, isn't it?

It's absolutely genius.

The strategy proved effective. Our children consistently forgot that the hidden toys ever existed.

As with all things good—such as our toy-removing strategy—Satan hijacks these ideas and uses them for his own diabolical benefit. In the same way that we hid toys from our children, the enemy attempts to hide our true

identity from us, to accomplish his goal of having the world
forget its destiny.

Our families are created by God to become living, breathing symbols of the Triune God, for the purpose of providing mankind with hope, with a link between heaven and
earth, with a reminder of our destiny and of the joy that
awaits us in heaven. The family's communion has been
created by God as a perpetual reminder of the eternal self-
giving love of the Trinity. The enemy's intent, however, is
to destroy the identity of the family and consequently keep
the family from achieving its destiny.

If our children are to one day live in heaven, heaven must
live on earth today. If the world is to one day experience
the eternal love of the Trinity, the Trinity must live in the
world today. The purpose of the family is to be the link
that connects our children, and the world, to their heavenly
homeland.

Family, Trinity, and Destiny

How do our families become like the Trinity? To become
like God, we must first know God. To become a symbol
of the Trinity, we need to know the Trinity. But what is
—who is—the Trinity?

We've heard the Trinity defined as "one God, three
Persons." But what does that really mean? The *Catechism*
explains it like this: "God has revealed His innermost secret:
God himself is an eternal exchange of love, Father, Son
and Holy Spirit, and he has destined us to share in that
exchange" (CCC 221).

God is essentially and eternally self-giving love. God
is three distinct Persons, who give themselves away to
one another so unreservedly that they are eternally and
essentially one. God desires for us to share in this exchange

of persons, this rapture, bliss, and union that will never end (CCC 1821).

Why is this truth important? The Trinity, the Father, Son, and Holy Spirit, are able to give themselves away to one another because they possess themselves, and this self-giving love produces life. The Trinity can be defined by its three main attributes: First, each divine Person is distinct, that is, each divine Person has an individual identity. Second, this distinction affords unity, that is, they share themselves fully with the other divine Persons. Third, the divine Persons of the Trinity, by means of this unity, are fruitful—that is, their union is so profound that God continually gives life.

This tells us that the more we master ourselves, the more capable we are of giving ourselves to another—particularly to our wives and children. And the more that we give ourselves away to our family, the more likely they will return themselves to us in self-giving love.

"[Man] cannot fully find himself except through a sincere gift of himself."[1] The family will only discover its identity as an icon of the Trinity when the members of the family give themselves away to one another. The human family is a created version of the Trinity, and is ordained by God to launch humanity into the uncreated reality of God. This is the purpose and meaning of our families.

Joseph's Family:
The Icon of the Trinity

St. Joseph's family, the Holy Family, was *the* icon of the Trinity, which had a human father who represented God the Father. Joseph's family was the first domestic church, whose example all other families are to follow.

Just as the Holy Family had Joseph as its leader, so also our families need us fathers to become the leaders and shepherds of our domestic churches.

Remember that the human father—by gathering his family to himself, thus gathering his family to God—images Christ, the high priest, who, at Holy Mass, gathers the human family to the Father. This indicates that the human father, like Christ, is the priest of his family.

But what is a priest and what does he do?

In a word, he offers himself in sacrifice on behalf of his wife and children that they may be holy. There are two basic characteristics of a father who is priest of his domestic church: secrecy and sacrifice.

Secrecy:
The Father's Secret

In the book *The Millionaire Next Door*, the authors, Thomas J. Stanley and William D. Danko, propose that quite often people who appear wealthy are in debt up to their noses, and those neighbors who generally appear to live modest, unassuming lives are the ones who have the bursting bank accounts and robust retirement plans. Whether or not this is true, the concept is very appealing.

The idea of the modest, unassuming character veiling a resilient, hidden hero is nothing new. Spider-Man, Superman, or Bill Bixby as the Hulk all had this fine quality of hidden strength. Perhaps that is why J.R.R. Tolkien's Hobbits, Frodo and Sam, are such magnetically appealing characters. Though small, modest, and apparently powerless, they carry an interior strength, and in fact, in Frodo's case, he carries the very power that will determine the destiny of Middle-earth.

Why didn't Tolkien select Aragorn, the ranger from the north, or Legolas, prince of the Elves, or Faramir to carry the terrible burden of Sauron's Ring of Power into Mount Doom? Though they all were warriors, experienced in battle, courageous, and physically resilient, they all lacked the essential key attribute of any great man—humility.

Humility is the foundation of all the virtues. It is the basis of a life of greatness, and in fact is almost synonymous with magnanimity, greatness of soul. Without humility, a man cannot wield God's power—the power to emulate and imitate the Father. The man who believes that he can, by himself, exert God's power is like Boromir, who pridefully believed that he could command the power of the One Ring. Rather than wielding such power, a man will be consumed by it.

Authentic fathers, whether we like it or not, are like Hobbits; we appear to be common folk, discreet, modest, regular, run-of-the-mill guys, but like Frodo, or like the millionaire next door, we have a power and richness within us that determines the fate of the world.

Why do we admire Peter Parker, Captain America, Frodo, or the modest millionaire? Perhaps we admire these characters because of their secrecy. They don't strut around flaunting their power. They don't boast about their conquests or share with everyone their latest successful endeavor. Quite the contrary: They veil their power. They do not cast their pearls before swine.

Jesus, the very Word of God, God the Son, did not arrive on our planet in a celestial cosmic electrical storm upon a fire-wheeled chariot, shooting lightning bolts from his divine eyeballs. Rather, his eternal creative power was veiled by His becoming a little, helpless infant who was dependent upon a young woman and her husband. In fact, the glorious event of Christ's Resurrection occurred in the secret of the silent, shadowed, dark, early Sunday morning hours. The most incredible, life-changing, soul-transforming event—a dead man definitively defeating sin and overcoming death bodily—was so sacred that it was accomplished in secret.

Life's most sacred and meaningful events are intended to occur in secret. Human beings are conceived in secret, men's sins are confessed to a priest in secret, and authentic fatherhood is accomplished in secret. It is that sacred.

Perhaps this is one of the reasons Jesus' silent years of living in Nazareth under the patronage of Joseph are veiled —because of their sacredness.

Why should fatherhood be accomplished in secret? Because that is how the heavenly Father lives His fatherhood. And we fathers are called to be icons of the heavenly Father, in order to transmit effectively His love to the world.

Our Lord revealed how human fathers are to imitate God the Father:

> "But when you give alms, do not let your left hand know what your right hand is doing, so that your alms may be given in secret; and your Father Who sees in secret, will reward you" (Matt. 6:3–4).

> "But when you pray, go into your room and shut the door and pray to your Father who is in secret; and your Father who sees in secret will reward you" (Matt. 6:6).

> "But when you fast, anoint your head and wash your face, that your fasting may not be seen by men but by your Father *who is in secret*; and your Father who sees in secret will reward you" (Matt. 6:17–18, emphasis added).

Jesus reveals that all of a father's actions should be motivated by the desire to perform these works for God alone—who sees in secret—rather than for the glory and praise of men.

But there is something else that our Lord reveals, something that is often overlooked. The reason for a father's secrecy is to imitate the "Father *who is in secret*." God the Father lives in secret, moves in secret, and blesses in secret —for He *is* in secret.

The works of God the Father are "glorious, and secret, and hidden" (Eccl. 11:4). From this we can conclude that the Father's secret to success is also the secret to every father's success, and that secret is secrecy itself.

Fatherhood is little, silent, and hidden. Fatherhood changes the world silently. A friend of mine likes to say that fatherhood is like the stud in the drywall. You can't see it but it holds up the drywall, the frame of the wall, the structure of the house. Fatherhood silently, secretly, holds up the structure of the family, the Church, and the world. Do you know what this means? You can tell your wife that you are a stud!

Three Ways to Work in Secret

Our Lord's words concerning secrecy reveal three truths, which, if embraced and lived, have the ability to radically transform our lives, our masculinity, and our fatherhood.

First, the fact that Jesus calls us to perform these works for the Father indicates that God desires us to collaborate with Him. As in the account of the wedding at Cana, God does not accomplish all of the work Himself, but rather, desires to work with us. Why does God want to work with us? One of the reasons is that the act of collaborating and working with God presupposes that we entrust to

Him our hopes, aspirations, and endeavors. God wants to fulfill these authentic desires and grant success to the work of our hands, in order to ensure that we experience His glory. But more importantly, by granting success to our voiced aspirations, God wants to demonstrate that He is our generous Father. To allow God to demonstrate that He is Father, it is imperative that we also demonstrate our trust in Him by offering our works to Him in a secret, nonboastful, noncomplaining manner.

Second, by acting in secrecy, we become real fathers. Our Lord tells us that by doing our works in secret we will become like our heavenly Father, "who is in secret." God accomplishes His greatest works secretly. God never boasts about His accomplishments or draws attention to Himself. In fact, our heavenly Father is so discreet that He is willing to allow atheists to say that He doesn't exist, while still sustaining them in existence. That's humility. That's greatness.

Third, if we labor with God in secret with the purpose of glorifying Him, He will also glorify us. It is a great paradox that by fulfilling the vocation of fatherhood in a secret and hidden manner that our fatherhood will be glorified. But recall the example of St. Joseph. St. Joseph was a most hidden father. In fact, as we've seen, Scripture does not record one single word spoken by him. Yet, today, Joseph is perhaps the most well-known father in history. How did this occur?

Joseph's fatherhood was revealed by means of his Son's life. Just as the hidden heavenly Father is made known by means of His Son, and as St. Joseph was revealed by means of his Son, so also, we fathers will be revealed by means of our children's lives.

The Son expressed the glory of both His secret heavenly Father, and the glory of His hidden earthly father, and our children will in some manner express the glory of our fatherhood. Love your children as they should love and they will love as they should.

A qualifier may be necessary. This does not mean that if your children rebel you are a bad father. Many fathers have been great fathers and nevertheless their children rebelled. However, many of those fathers endured their children's rebellion heroically. Even if a child strays from the path of virtue, a good father will be known by how he persevered in loving his child despite their rebellion.

But so often, we exchange the life of masculine, secret, self-sacrificial love for the lauds and affirmation of others. We sell ourselves and our true identity out. This dynamic is so prevalent that in Protestant circles it is defined as PK (Pastor's Kid) Syndrome. In those cases, the pastor, who is also a father, applies himself to his occupation as a pastor, believing that he is accomplishing the Lord's work, while he inadvertently neglects his children. Eventually, his children lose their faith in the heavenly Father because they lost their faith in their human father.

Recently, a woman shared the all-too-common account of a husband who became a pillar in his church community, led RCIA programs, organized men's retreats, hosted Bible studies, facilitated prayer groups, and the list went on. Despite all his efforts to reach his church community and renew the Church, his own children lost their faith. When children lose the intimate love of their human father, they also often conclude that the heavenly Father does not love them. The optimal way of renewing the macro Church is by revitalizing the micro church of the family. This effort should be at the heart of the New Evangelization.

Secret Works Work

Now, perhaps in the back of your mind a question is nagging you: How can works performed secretly make any real impact? No one, at least on a grand scale, will see the good works, and therefore no one will be aware of them, and therefore no one will be inspired by them. Right?

It does appear that way, but let's examine how secret works work.

Clouds are known to contain hundreds of thousands of gallons of water. It's as though a lake is floating overhead. These tremendously large water sources are hidden, yet exist in plain sight. In order for clouds to develop, the dew from the fields, moisture from the seas and oceans, mist contained in the air—all imperceptible to the human eye—rise into the atmosphere and, over time, collect, eventually becoming clouds. These clouds gather into larger cloud formations, eventually releasing rain upon the earth—rain that brings forth fruits and bountiful harvests.

A father's works are like the mist in the air and the moisture from the seas, which if offered consistently—without boasting or complaining, and with the intention of glorifying God—will be gathered by God, who eventually by His divine command orders that they shower graces upon humanity.

Our works, though accomplished with the motive of being secretly given to God, are like clouds hidden in plain sight. We simply perform these acts so discreetly, and with the proper motivation, that they are almost imperceptible to those around us.

For example, a friend shared with me the story of his father, who died recently. After his death, his family discovered in his Bible a long list of prayer intentions, many of which had been miraculously answered. Though no one knew of this during his lifetime, his secret sacrificial love became known.

Steve, a friend of mine, a very compassionate, loving man, died on Valentine's Day after a routine outpatient surgery. Steve had a huge heart. At the end of the funeral Mass, his daughters addressed the assembled crowd, saying that their dad loved them, and showed them love in many ways, but most importantly, by loving their mom. Those two daughters testified that they desired to marry men who had the qualities their father had. Steve accomplished his fatherhood in a secret, discreet manner, which became known to his entire church community. Truly, as our Lord says, what is hidden will be revealed.

We fathers should be listening to their testimony. We need to become the father that we want our daughters to marry, and we need to become the father that we want our sons to be.

Sacrificial Love

A father sets the pace of self-giving love. Typically, he can expect his children to love at the level that he loves. As Christ tells us, "A disciple is not above his teacher, but every one when he is fully taught will be like his teacher" (Luke 6:40). A father is called to be the teacher of his children by becoming the priest of his family. A priest is someone who offers sacrifices.

Sacrifice is derived from two Latin words, "*sacer*" (sacred) and "*facere*" (to make), and can be interpreted as "to make holy." When we sacrifice something, we set it aside for God, and in doing so, it becomes holy. But what does a father set aside in order for God to make it holy? What does he offer to God?

He offers himself.

A father sets aside his ego, his disordered desires, the many burning temptations to selfish love, all for the sake of his family and his God. We, like the Magi who visited the infant Jesus in Bethlehem, offer to our Lord gold, frankincense, and myrrh.

The gold is the money that we gain by means of our labors. We choose to set the money aside, offering it to God, by not spending it so much on ourselves, as on our ministry —our family. We offer frankincense, that is, prayers for our wife and children, for their growth in holiness, health, and success. We offer myrrh, that is, we die to our selfish will with the purpose of leading by serving and serving in order to lead.

Recall that the family is an icon of the self-giving, eternal exchange of Persons in the Trinity. Also remember that the father is called to set the pace of self-giving love. In order for our families to become icons of the Trinity, we ought to lead by serving. If we expect our children to become great leaders, it is important that they learn to follow someone great—that is, that we should be that great leader by serving in humility.

"The greater you are, the more you must humble yourself: so you will find favor in God" (Sir. 3:18). "For every one who exalts himself will be humbled, and he who humbles himself will be exalted" (Luke 14:11).

Humility is obtained by means of embracing humiliations. Humiliations are often the result of being misunderstood by another, misunderstanding another, being rejected by another, making an error, having a fault exposed, or committing a sin. These humiliations have an uncanny way of piercing our disordered ego with pinpoint accuracy. Ironically, a multitude of humiliations will occur precisely within the context of family life, and amidst our efforts to build the domestic church.

Rather than the domestic church being a place of refuge from humiliations, it is the place of purification by means of humiliations. Don't shoot the messenger. It happens to me as well. But why does it have to be this way?

The more we draw closer to those around us, particularly our immediate family members, the more vulnerable we become, and the more our true self—all the good and all the bad—is revealed. For example, there are very few people who will have the glorious opportunity to encounter me upon arising, complete with my typically overpowering halitosis and alarming case of bedhead. Yet, in my vulnerability, my family bears that burden. There are also very few people who have to endure my impatience or biting tongue, as my family does.

Our vulnerability among those we love offers the opportunity for us to be loved despite our faults.

Being the generous man that I am, I offer my family an ongoing multitude of opportunities to grow in love, giving them occasions to love me despite my faults.

The tendency in all of us is to blame others, criticize others, complain about others, condemn other's actions, or have contempt for them. As fathers, it is imperative that we refrain from blaming, criticizing, complaining, condemning, or become contemptuous, lest our children grow to become like us.

A father who is humble is capable of bearing the burdens of his family members with love. This could mean helping with the dishes after dinner, or changing a diaper when you want to watch the game. The key is to have a "vision for charity," and begin seeing the many ways that we can serve. When we see the opportunity to serve, we will also be confronted with the temptation to serve the self by fleeing from or avoiding the sacrifice. It is during these opportunities to serve that if we offer ourselves to God without complaint, our act of service becomes sacrificial, an offering set aside for God.

Having a special-needs fourteen-year-old daughter, who as we've seen is confined to a wheelchair and will wear diapers for the rest of her life, has offered many unique opportunities to serve. Let's be honest. Who, after coming home from a full day at the office, thinks, "Great! It's my turn to change the diaper!" But that is precisely the moment when a sacrifice becomes an act of love—when we move beyond our fleshly desires to a desire to serve for the sake of the other, especially when we don't want to sacrifice.

Several years ago, as I was changing one of Anna Marie's awful diapers, I began resenting my lot in life. A couple of days later, while unloading Anna Marie from the van, I lifted her incorrectly and ruptured several of the lower discs in my spine. As I was rehabilitating and undergoing physical therapy, I watched my daughters and wife bear the burden of caring for Anna Marie without my assistance. At one point I prayed to God, asking Him to heal me so that I could help care for my little Anna again. It was during that time that I discovered a truth: I don't *have* to serve Anna Marie. I *get* to serve Anna Marie. Serving her is a gift.

A friend of mine, whose daughter committed suicide, said that he would give nearly anything to be with his daughter for only seven more days. Do you think that during those seven days he would feel as though he *had* to serve her, or would he believe it an honor to serve her?

When our children see their father bearing their burdens or their mother's burdens with love, they will more likely reciprocate that love and offer themselves in service to their family. It takes time and effort and patience and humility. If we are willing to set the pace of self-giving love, our family will most likely follow that pace, and doing so, remind this world that the Trinity exists, is real, and is our destiny.

Accepting Criticism, Making Mistakes, and Forgiveness

Fresh out of college, I began my art career with a slight, almost imperceptible ego (it was enormous). I believed that I was someone very, very special, a major art talent, who was above being criticized. I learned quickly that if I wanted to actually be good at my job, it was vital to humble myself and learn from those who were more experienced.

Initially, the experience of being criticized was painful, like massaging myself with a cheese grater. On one occasion, my client, after viewing an online presentation containing several book cover options, asked me if I had been drunk the night before I designed the covers. Responding that I hadn't, he then said, "Are you sure? It looks like you vomited all over the computer screen." Yes, like massaging oneself with a cheese grater, criticisms sting.

But over time, I learned to savor the critique and the advice, because I discovered that as I listened and acted upon them, I became better at my job.

It can be like that in family life. If we, as fathers, believe ourselves to be above criticism and become upset, pouty, or resentful when a family member (particularly our wives) corrects us, we can expect our children to behave in the same manner. If, however, we can receive correction humbly—without being a doormat—we and our family members will grow in trust, communion, and character. In other words, our families will become icons of the Trinity.

Several years ago, I took two of my daughters, aged five and six, sledding. Each of them had their own sled and after each trip down the hill they would complete their turn by asking if I could come down to help them back up the hill. After doing this several times, I decided to try a more efficient approach. I decided to pack the three of us into a single sled, thinking that by being with them, I would only have to trek up the hill once and then begin again.

The girls giggled and laughed as I jammed them onto that little sled. With their interests in mind, I was determined to have this be the fastest sled ride ever. I made a running start, jumped in, and I launched us from the top of the hill. I loved it. The girls were screaming. I was laughing. And then it happened. We hit a bump, the sled flipped in midair, and within moments my daughters were buried in the snow with their father on top of them.

The crying ensued. Tears were trickling from their snow-packed faces. It was a long, miserable, return trek up the hill to the car—where my wife was seated in heated luxury. After explaining what I had done, my wife asked the $64,000 question: "Devin, do you think that was a good idea?" Though it was cold outside, I was boiling on the inside. Eventually, I realized that perhaps it wasn't a good idea to sled down the hill at such an accelerated pace.

Mistakes will be made. Some mistakes are small, like tipping the sled, but some mistakes loom larger and can alter our lives permanently.

An acquaintance of mine, Jay, was watching his eighteen-month-old son in his backyard. For only a moment, he took his eyes off of him. It was just enough time for the child to leave the yard, while Jay's sixteen-year-old daughter was backing the car out of the driveway. She backed over the little boy. As Jay held the dead body of his son, he had enough wherewithal to embrace his daughter simultaneously. Jay lost a son that day, but he refused to also lose his daughter.

Jay never blamed his daughter for his son's death, but instead endured the trial with her. Together they grieved their loss. Jay's love and forgiveness was so tender that his daughter forgave herself, eventually married, had her own child, and in that child, Jay and his daughter rejoiced— and still rejoice. Today, Jay says through tears, "I think that event has taught me how much God the Father loves us and forgives us, despite what we've done to His Son."

Forgiveness is the heart of the domestic church, and is essential for a family who loves like the Trinity. An old friend, Nathan, would often recount the occasion when his father, who was a politician, summoned his eight sons to an important family meeting. Of the eight, seven of his sons were present to witness their father humbling himself and asking forgiveness for living for his career rather than living for them. All his sons—with the exception of the son who was absent—eventually returned to their Catholic faith.

One of the essential attributes of a great father is that he is willing to humble himself and ask his wife and children for forgiveness. Asking for forgiveness is not simply saying the words "I'm sorry." By saying "I'm sorry," we are maintaining control of the situation. By saying, rather, "Will you forgive me?" we surrender our heart into the other's possession, granting them the ability to release us from our guilt. A father who does this will most often be profoundly respected by his children.

Recall that if our children are to one day live in heaven, heaven must live on earth today. If the world is to one day experience the trinitarian eternal exchange of love, the Trinity must live in the world today. Your family is a link that connects your children with their heavenly homeland. It is the human father who connects the family and the Trinity.

By becoming the priest of your domestic church, offering sacrifice in secrecy, you will aid your family in achieving its eternal destiny.

SECRET 7

BUILD AND BLESS

Thriving or Surviving

It was nearly two and a half years after the birth of Anna Marie, and my wife and I, and the doctors, could not project how her brain injury would affect her cognitive and motor skills, her ability to function.

Around this time, Jim, a family friend, invited us to his daughter's first birthday. When the time arrived for his daughter, who was sitting upright on the floor, to open her gifts, Jim called his daughter over to him. She proceeded to crawl on all fours, and then pushed herself into a standing position, from which she proceeded to walk, with Frankenstein-like motion, to her father. We all clapped and cheered with excitement, as this was one of the first occasions that Jim's daughter had walked.

While smiling externally, I was tormented internally. I couldn't avoid comparing Jim's one-year-old walking daughter to my two-and-a-half-year-old Anna Marie, who at that moment was sitting on the floor, with her back braced and lodged between my lower legs to assist her in maintaining a sitting position.

Anna Marie could not sit up on her own; she would simply tip over. Why was it that after two and a half years, Anna Marie was unable to sit up on her own? Why couldn't she crawl? Would she ever walk, sit up, or even crawl?

Pained, angry, and emotionally crushed, I left Jim's house thinking to myself, "Devin, she has permanent brain injury. What did you expect?" I expected the best. I expected that Anna Marie would snap out of it, come to her senses, and figure out how to make her body do what it was created to do.

I had determined that before bedtime Anna Marie would crawl. After we arrived home from the party, I laid her on the floor, and stepping backward a couple of feet in front of her, began to coax her, encouraging her to crawl to me.

Nothing happened.

Again, I called her by name, peppering her with phrases like "You can do it" and "You've got it in you," pleading with her to crawl to me. She reared her head back and attempted to move her arms, but no progress was made. Determined that something as simple as crawling can be learned easily, I continued to coax and coach her, hoping with every bit of my soul that she would demonstrate some sign of bodily control.

But nothing happened.

Becoming angry and impatient, I laid beside her and manually moved her arms and legs in an army crawl motion, saying to her, "Anna, this is how you crawl." My emotions, the feeling of hopelessness, the realization that I had no control of the situation, got the best of me.

As I lay beside her, exasperated emotionally, with my face buried in my hands, a truth pierced my soul: "Devin, do you see how you desire that your daughter crawl so much that you lay beside her, attempting to do it for her? Just as you want her to crawl, I want both you and her not only to crawl, but to walk with Me, and in order to accomplish this, I not only come beside you, but in you. Yes, I am inside of you, not only that you may walk but fly."

In that moment, I received an incredible insight: God doesn't simply want His children to survive, He wants us to live, to walk, to fly with Him, and He accomplishes this by condescending to our level.

We are all spiritually handicapped. We are all are spiritually special-needs kids. God does not abandon us in our condition, but rather, He became one of us, in order that He could live in us and make our weak, handicapped souls strong, vital, and powerful. This is the point of the Word becoming man. By becoming one of us, God is encouraging us to trust in His love, to open ourselves to his Spirit, and to allow the Holy Spirit to transform our weaknesses into supernatural strength.

Quite often, opening ourselves to the Holy Spirit can be painful. Consider that a balloon without air is useless and flat, but when air is pumped into its elastic shell, its skin stretches, allowing the balloon to achieve the purpose for which it has been designed. But notice that in order for the balloon to achieve its full potential, it has to endure the painful process of being stretched, and the more it is stretched, the more air it contains, until it is capable of soaring aloft.

Human beings are like balloons. Without the breath of the Holy Spirit, we are flat, lifeless, and do not achieve the purpose for which we have been created—to soar with God. By opening ourselves to the breath of the Holy Spirit, we move from merely existing to actually living. Opening ourselves to "containing" more of the Holy Spirit demands that our souls be stretched, which at times can be quite painful.

When the Spirit of God enters us, it stretches us, calling us to do things that initially seem painful, unattractive, and inconvenient. This stretching usually involves the lowering of ourselves to serve those around us. Paradoxically, to

soar with God is dependent upon lowering ourselves—
particularly to serve our children. Indeed, "he who is least
among you all is the one who is great" (Luke 9:48).

After that birthday party, I physically lowered myself
to Anna Marie's level, and in doing so I was allowed to
experience not only Anna Marie's lowliness, weakness, and
dependence, but my own lowliness, weakness, and utter
dependence upon God. Like Anna Marie, I was helpless.
We were helpless together. That day I learned one of the
keys to heroic fatherhood: to share our children's plights
as though they are our own. This is precisely what God
the Father does for each of us.

The Holy Spirit enables us to soar by inspiring us to
lower ourselves to the level of serving our children. The
Holy Spirit will enable our children to soar if we lower
ourselves to serve them.

It is probably safe to say that none of us want our children
to merely survive this thing we call life; we want them to
live. To ensure that our children live truly, it is imperative
that we die to our selfishness so that we can truly live and
pass on life. Many fathers say that they would die for their
children, but how many men truly live for their children?
If we want our children to experience the vitality that God
can offer, it is imperative that we fathers become a conduit,
a reservoir, that transmits and pours out the blessing of God
the Father upon our children.

Building and Blessing

Often the world's strife, rebellion, and pride streams from
ruptured relationships between fathers and their children.
Division between a child and his father can often instill
resentment in the child, causing a child to deny the blessing
that he inherits from his father and become preoccupied

with making a name for himself—that is, building himself into a god.

This dynamic has been prevalent since the beginning of human history. Recall the motive of the people who built the Tower of Babel: "Come, let us build ourselves a city, and a tower with its top in the heavens, and let us make a name for ourselves, lest we be scattered abroad upon the face of the whole earth" (Gen. 11:4). The plan, on the surface, sounds innocent enough; they wanted a strong, fortified city with a tower with an awe-inspiring lookout.

We, however, know the rest of the story: "[T]he LORD scattered them abroad from there over the face of all the earth, and they left off building the city. Therefore its name was called Babel, because there the LORD confused the language of all the earth" (Gen. 11:8–9). Why would God scatter the people of Shinar, permanently ending the project of building the city and the tower? We need to understand the backstory in order to understand why this endeavor failed.

Noah had three sons, Ham, Shem, and Japheth. Ham was the son who found Noah, his father, drunk and uncovered (naked) in his tent, and exposed his father's shame to his brothers. Ham's two brothers obtained a cover, walked backward into the tent, and laid the cover over their father's nakedness. Noah, upon awakening, discovered "what Ham had done unto him," and consequently cursed Ham's son, Canaan, and his bloodline. In the same breath, Shem, whose name means "name" or "fame," received Noah's fatherly blessing.

The ruler of the Kingdom of Babel was Ham's grandson, Nimrod, who, being the son of Canaan, inherited Noah's curse.

Nimrod and the descendants of Canaan attempted to build a "Shem"—a name—for themselves in order to prove that they could build a kingdom that would rival Shem's kingdom—a kingdom that would reach heaven without heaven's God, that would reach the Fatherland without the Father's blessing.

The lesson is clear: children who do not receive a blessing from their fathers in some form can become resentful and rebellious, and attempt to build a temple of self-absorption, rather than allowing themselves to be formed into a temple of God. This type of building project also ends in tragedy.

Just as strife and discord between Noah the father and Ham the son led to the eventual demise of Babel, so also such tension between fathers and their children can cause confusion, disharmony, and resentment in their relationship —and consequently cause a child to resent God the Father.

The Three Stages of Building and Blessing

The account of the Tower of Babel reveals the existence of an inherently powerful relationship between blessing and building—between the human father's blessing and how the child builds his life. In other words, if a child is to be built into a temple of God, it is imperative that the child have his father's blessing.

A father is called by God to bless his child in order to help his child be built into a temple of the Holy Spirit. A father blesses in order to build, and builds in order to bless. He blesses his children in order that they be built into temples of God, so that they may bless God, and those whom their lives touch; and he works with God in building himself into a temple of God in order that his blessing be effective.

There are three basic stages to blessing our children so that they may become temples of the living God. First, a father is to identify his child as a temple of God—God's dwelling place. Second, a father is to give to his child the materials needed in order for him to fulfill this project. Third, a father is to charge his child to build the temple of God in his person, which is accomplished by imparting on the child the fatherly blessing. To fulfill these three stages, we fathers are to become the voice, the face, and the touch of the heavenly Father. In other words, we are to teach our children the lesson of authentic self-giving love. However, in attempting to become an effective teacher of self-donation we will encounter the tenacious temptation of selfishness.

Recall that a father's mission is to be a link between heaven and earth, between God and His children, and he accomplishes this by becoming the voice of the Father that our children cannot hear, the face of the Father that our children cannot see, and the touch of the Father that our children cannot feel.

This threefold manner of communicating love to our children is precisely the way that God the Father communicates His love to us: "That which was from the beginning, which we have heard, which we have seen with our eyes, which we looked upon and touched with our hands, concerning the word of life . . . that you may have fellowship . . . with his Son Jesus Christ" (1 John 1:1–3).

God the Father communicated His very Word, His very life, to us in Jesus' physical presence—in Jesus' voice, Jesus' face, and Jesus' very touch.

By becoming the voice, the face, and the touch of the Father, we are fulfilling our role as teacher to our children and overcome the temptation to selfishness.

Identifying the Temple:
Becoming the Voice of the Father

Our children, though appearing to be common, fallen, inexperienced adolescents, are more than the eye perceives. The human child is an outward sign that directs people, particularly fathers, to an interior mystery expressed from within them. Every baptized child is a temple of God, a temple of the Holy Spirit, a dwelling place of God in the making.

By means of sharing with our children life's vital lessons, words of encouragement, words of correction, but most important, the knowledge that God dwells within them, we become the voice of the Father, the voice that transmits these truths to our children. Our words are at the service of a singular goal: to help our children understand that they are temples of the living God, and that this is their very identity, dignity, and honor.

Now, it should go without saying that believing our visible children to be temples of the invisible God is perhaps one of the greatest challenges of fatherhood, and truly demands great faith.

Mary, a neighbor who lives down the street, enjoys recounting the story of her five-year-old grandson David, whose seven-year-old brother woke his father at 3 A.M. with the news, "Dad, David and I have been up all night. Dad, David ate your contacts." David's Dad responded, "Well, it was time for new ones anyway."

John, a friend of mine, has a daughter, Michelle, who has Down syndrome and attended public school for the first time last year. Typically, Michelle would spend most of her time playing quietly in the back of the kinder-garten classroom. One afternoon, while she was playing, her teacher was writing on the chalkboard attentively, attempting to teach the children how to write their letters. When she turned around to face the class, she discovered that Michelle was standing on her desk, arms outstretched—buck naked.

Indeed, sometimes it can be difficult to discern the dignity of the divine in these little creatures we call children. The central tenets of our faith, such as belief in grace, existence of a Triune God, the reality of heaven and hell, the power of the Holy Spirit, the resurrection of the body, and angels and demons, demand great faith. But, among these, often none demand as great a faith than believing that a child is a temple of God. "Blessed are those who have not seen and yet believe" (John 20:29).

How difficult it is for a father to see and believe that God lives in his child when his child is addicted to drugs, suffering from alcoholism or anorexia, or is stealing from the family to feed an addiction.

But it is then, perhaps more than at any other time, that our children need us fathers to see God in them.

Considering this, lack of faith in the reality that a child is a temple of God can often lead to abuse or neglect of the child—either by indulging and spoiling the child, or by failing to encourage or inspire the child, or by a lack of real investment in the child.

Nearly every disordered parenting tendency is rooted in a lack of belief that the child is a sacred dwelling place of God.

Words Have Power

Sean, now thirty-seven years of age, throughout his childhood was continually and consistently drilled by his father with the message that he was a "stupid good for nothin' who would amount to nothin'." Sean's dad did not see his goodness or potential, and certainly did not see God in his son. Sean has recently been incarcerated, for the third time, at a state penitentiary, with a twenty-year sentence. The words spoken by his father were a curse rather than a blessing. The words of a father, whether he realizes it or not, can have prophetic power.

Recently, a young man, eighteen years of age, shared with me that throughout his childhood, his father would taunt him, call him fat, tell him that he was a boy and would never be a man. While he was speaking his chin began to shake, his voice trembled, and his lips quivered as he attempted to suppress the tears.

Why does it hurt? Why does the pain penetrate the human person so deeply? When a child is belittled and demeaned by his father, his inner person is cut, his heart bleeds, and in the deep and dark caverns of his soul exists a wound that few will ever encounter—because most likely he won't let anyone in. To do so would require that he become vulnerable, and he understands that vulnerability is precisely what allowed him to become so deeply wounded.

Why does it hurt? Because the human father is the trans-mitter, the icon, the very symbol of the heavenly Father, and when a child is demeaned by his father he cannot help but believe that the heavenly Father's sentiments are the same.

On the other hand, if we openly convey the truth to our children that they are temples of the Holy Spirit, they will more readily strive to achieve this reality. Tell your child that he is good and he most likely will become good. When a father verbally communicates the goodness of his child to his child, he is instilling a certain confidence in his child, while also building the child's confidence in their relationship, which often, consequently, builds the child's trust in the heavenly Father.

My wife's friend Elizabeth shared an account from her high school days, when she and her friends were planning a trip to the beach. Elizabeth asked her dad if she could wear a two-piece swimsuit, since all of her friends would be wearing them. Her father simply said no, and that was the end of the conversation. Elizabeth was fuming, enraged and humiliated. What would her friends think? She would be the only one of them not wearing a two-piece.

Regardless, Elizabeth obeyed her father and trekked down to the beach in her wrestling singlet.

Later, after the fallout had settled, Elizabeth's dad took her aside and privately explained to her that she was beautiful—too beautiful to have her dignity and feminine glory unveiled and thrown before the swine of hormone-infested boys who couldn't love and respect her in the manner worthy of her inner dignity and feminine mystery.

Elizabeth's father, in his own way, communicated to her that she is a temple of God—holy and beautiful— and should be revered as such. Today, Elizabeth says with tremendous pride, "I am so glad that my father loved me enough to give me self-respect." It is imperative that we communicate to our children "You are made for more," rather than "You are good for nothing." If we do not openly communicate to them that they are temples of God, who will?

The Most Important Words

One of the most important messages we fathers can give to our children is that they are unique gifts. Children practically come forth from the womb picking dandelions for mom and drawing pictures for dad. I have a rock collection comprised of the many pebbles and stones that my children, from their earliest years, have given to me. In addition to that, I have boxes full of cards, poems, drawings, and notes that were created by my children specifically for me.

What's the point? Why do children behave like this? Because they are created by God to be a gift and to share themselves with those whom they love.

Often, this giftedness is overlooked by a parent, or brushed aside, or worse, immediately discarded into the trash can. Now, I'm not recommending that we store every note, drawing, and trinket that our children give to us. But we should immediately acknowledge the gift, honor the gift, and receive the gift—for by doing so, we communicate to our children that we acknowledge, honor, and receive them as the true gift. This is a crucial point. It is imperative that we congratulate and affirm our children every time they attempt to be a gift—especially when it falls short— lest they refrain from being a gift because there is no one to receive the gift of themselves being presented in their gifts.

The act of affirming our children in their giftedness is as simple as thanking your son for being kind to his sister, or thanking your daughter for setting the table, or congratulating your child for her efforts at school. It could be as simple as affirming your child for his witty sense of humor, or your daughter for her beauty, both interior and exterior, or for simply being who he or she truly is— unique and unrepeatable.

These types of affirmations communicate the message that you notice your children and that they are important to you. Your children desire to be noticed, to be important, and if you don't provide this type of affirmation, they will try to obtain it elsewhere.

By receiving and affirming our children and their unique giftedness, they will desire to become more of a gift, and by giving themselves away, they will discover more of their identity. And discovering their identity they will discover their destiny.

Assisting our children in their giftedness unlocks them from selfishness and affords them the freedom of a life of self-giving love. I truly wonder if there is anything as effective in raising children as recognizing their unique, individual giftedness.

One of the most effective ways in which we can become the voice of the Father is by audibly expressing, in some manner, this truth: "Do you not know that your body is a temple of the Holy Spirit within you, which you have from God?" (1 Cor. 6:19). If this truth is transmitted without manipulation or coercion, our children will be granted true confidence in, and reverence for, themselves—a reverence that enables them to become virtuous, noble, and full of character. When a father communicates the truth to his child that God lives within him, that child has an instinctive desire to live up to that reality. The human father is the voice of the Father that our children cannot hear.

Giving the Materials:
Becoming the Face of the Father

After we have identified our children as temples of the Holy Spirit, it is vital that we give them the materials to continue to build that temple. The time of providing materials is a season of preparation, a period of training, in which a father builds the child's trust and confidence in God the Father by building that trust between his child and himself.

The human father accomplishes this by being the face of the Father to his child, that is, he makes himself present to his child. When we make ourselves present to our children, we become a "present," a gift that transmits the presence of the Father to our children. When we make ourselves present to our children, they begin to believe that they are worthy of our time. By being present, we give our children by means of our example—over and above our words—the much-needed materials to be built into temples of God.

There are two fundamental errors a father can make in giving his child the materials to build the temple of God in himself. A father can burden his child, by placing expectations upon him beyond what he is capable of fulfilling. This premature pressure can cause "spiritual burnout," resentment for the faith, or worse, a rejection of the person of Jesus Christ.

The other extreme is to allow the years of training and preparation to slip by unnoticed, until one day the child sets out on his own without any real sense of mission, and without comprehending that the key to true happiness is found in self-giving love.

The Season Is Slipping By

My neighbor's sixteen-year-old daughter, Bella, was a very shy, beautiful young lady. She had gorgeous thick black hair, and a smooth, Asian complexion. She was academically astute, sweet, attractive. Altogether, she was striking.

The lamp in Bella's bedroom window, located on the second story on the front of the house, would often shine like a beacon into the late evening darkness.

One day, before sunrise on a cold, December morning, I noticed the flashing lights of several police cars parked in front of their house. Though I was curious about why police were at my neighbor's house so early in the morning, I thought it would be best to mind my own business and not ask any questions.

I noticed that after that bitter December morning, the lamp in Bella's room stopped shining. What I didn't know was that the beacon of Bella's light had been permanently extinguished—

She had committed suicide.

Her beautiful light would never pierce the world's cold darkness again.

Bella had been bullied at school, intimidated because of her beauty and her reserved character. She was told that she was weird, different, and was mocked in her social circles to the point where she could not endure the torture any longer.

I wanted to reach out to Bella's parents, but I felt helpless. What could I say? What could I do? Nothing could remove the pain, the anguish, the torment of their loss. I purchased some food and flowers and mustered enough courage to visit them.

I was scared and a bit nervous as I knocked on their door. Bella's mom, who was normally very reserved, answered the door, welcomed me inside, and without saying a word, stretched her arms wide, gesturing for me to embrace her. Then she fell into my arms, shaking and sobbing. Bella's father entered the room and he, too, collapsed into my arms, and both of them together, with their faces buried in my shoulders, wept like little children while clinging to me.

After crying together, Bella's father fixed his gaze intently upon me, and without blinking said, "Devin, hold on to your girls. Time is fleeting. They are so precious and the time you have with them is so limited. The world chews them up and spits them out. What we see as virtue the world views as weakness."

The time that we have with our children is slipping by, never to return. It is vital that we use this time wisely by being actively present to our children.

There are several ways that we can do that, and become the face of the Father that they cannot see. We will focus on three: look, listen, and touch.

First, a father should actually look into his child's eyes, often, and see into his or her soul. By stopping what you are doing and engaging your child face-to-face, you are transmitting your very presence to your child, your attention, and the message that he or she is more important than the task at hand. Realistically, this cannot happen all the time. Rather, it should be present in our minds, so that we strive to make every effort to do this as often as we can.

Second, a father should listen—not just hear, but actively listen. It is important to listen to what is *not* being said as much as to what *is* being said. My daughter may tell me that things are going well, but if I do not stop what I am doing and look into her eyes and listen to her, I may miss the hidden message: Dad, I'm struggling at school. Dad, I feel like a failure. Dad, is something wrong with me? I don't fit in. Dad, is it normal to be really attracted to boys? Dad—you fill in the blank.

The more we stop and actively listen, the more our children will entrust us with their hearts.

Steve, a friend of mine, recounted a moment when his teenage daughter was attempting to discuss something important with him. His mind was preoccupied, and "faking it," he asked a question, acting as though he was listening, but the question didn't quite relate to the subject at hand. His daughter painfully implored him, "Dad! You're not listening." Our children have radar that can detect whether dad is authentically listening or simply pretending to be interested. We often want our children to listen to us, but it is just as important, if not more important, that we listen to them. Our children will care to know when they know we care.

It is important to enter our children's world and express our interest in them in the manner in which we desire the Father to be interested in us. Imagine pouring out your latest crisis at work or trouble in your marriage to God, only to discover that the Father is snoring or watching the Bears game. You probably wouldn't feel like the "chosen son."

It is important that we ask the right questions and refrain from talking over our children, monologing or preaching at them. It is not so much *what* we say to our children that will aid them, as much as *how well* we listen to them. If we listen to them, they will be far more apt to listen to us.

But don't worry—even if they don't appear to be listening, they are watching. As a young teen, Mason said to his father, "I listen to 50 percent of what you say, and 100 percent of what you do." We should not be concerned that our children are not always listening, but rather be more concerned that they are always watching.

Karol Wojtyła recounted the fact that after his mother and older brother died, he and his father slept in the same room. Often Karol would awake in the middle of the night to see his father kneeling on the floor, praying just as he did at church. Karol said, "We never spoke about a vocation to the priesthood, but his example was in a way my first seminary, a kind of domestic seminary."[1] Karol eventually became St. John Paul II.

When our children see that God is our top priority, they will be more likely to make God their top priority. It is essential that our children see us going to Holy Mass, frequenting Holy Communion and the sacrament of confession, leading prayer at meals, praying the rosary, and sharing Sacred Scripture with the family. Indeed, our example is far more powerful than lectures. As the saying goes, your life may be the only Bible your children will ever read.

Recently, a father described how he and his teenage son had grown distant, and the father began to feel an incredible tension in their relationship. The father, understanding that he needed to address the problem, decided to take his son to lunch and find out why he was becoming resentful and defiant. The conversation fizzled and in desperation the father asked his son, "When was the last time it was good between us?" The son responded, "When you wanted to be with me."

Then he proceeded to vividly recount the specific event that he considered the last time his father truly wanted to be with him.

By being present to our children, we communicate the message, "I want to be with you."

Work as an Expression of Love

Recall that it is a father's duty to teach his child how to love, how to become a gift. The primary method of teaching a child to love is to work side by side with the child, teaching the child to work within the context of the family—for the sake of the family. Work has been redeemed and transformed into a way of making us holy by Christ, the carpenter (Mark 6:3), who was the son of the carpenter (Matt. 13:55), who faithfully worked at Joseph's side, learning the value and meaning of work. This indicates that familial work has been given the power to perfect us by Christ's own work.

The modern American family has been blessed with temporal riches, technological benefits, and comforts and luxuries not known to previous generations. Often, because of these benefits, we forget the glory and even the necessity of work as a means of educating our children to grow in self-giving love.

Familial work offers a way for our children to participate in family life by using their abilities, gifts, and talents, and by doing so, our children discover more of their particular identity. As the Church proclaims, "[Man] cannot fully find himself except through a sincere gift of himself."[2] Within the context of familial work, the child can discover how to work selflessly for the sake of others, rather than for selfish gain. The child will likely follow the example of parents who sacrifice themselves in little ways by cleaning, home maintenance, cooking, yard work, planting, sewing, building, farming, all without receiving a wage—all for the sake of the family.

A father who serves his children will naturally teach his children to serve. When children learn this lesson of self-donation, the burdens of life are shared, love is exchanged, persons are given to one another, talents are discovered, and the child learns to give himself as a gift to those around him.

Now, in case any clarification is needed, a father cannot be the only servant, but is obligated to teach his children how to participate in sharing the work. Likewise, a child cannot be a slave, but should learn to work side by side with his father.

Training a child to participate in familial work is indispensable and demands patience in bearing with the child's inexperience. But if such inexperience is endured patiently, a child will eventually learn to willingly offer himself to assist others.

To exercise such patience can pose a great challenge to the human father. During a recent winter, my home state, Iowa, received a record-setting amount of snowfall.

Shoveling the walks that winter was almost as routine as going to the bathroom. My seven-year-old daughter was constantly asking if she could help with the snow removal. Any experienced snow shoveler will tell you that if your seven-year-old comes out to help, she is simply going to trounce all over the snow, pack it down, and create more work for you. But I had to keep in mind that it is not about getting the work done right, as much as it is about working next to my child. A child working by her dad's side is one of the greatest weapons used to conquer selfishness and idleness, while also helping the child discover that she is needed, useful, wanted, and a gift to the family—especially to daddy.

Joseph and Jesus: Work as an Expression of Love

According to St. John Paul II, "Work was the daily expression of love in the life of the Family of Nazareth."[3] Joseph blessed Jesus with an environment for the perfect Son of God to perfect human nature through mutual self-giving —within Joseph the carpenter's workshop.

Joseph worked with Jesus and for Jesus, who worked with Joseph and for Joseph. Joseph, by means of work, trained Jesus in the art of self-donation, and in doing so, Joseph was trained in that same art. Indeed, raising a child raises a man.

Working, sweating, conversing, sharing ideas and burdens, Joseph trained his Son, by means of self-sacrificial love, for His project of building the temple of sacrifice in His person. Within the humble carpenter's workshop, Joseph and Jesus crafted the cross of self-giving love by means of sharing themselves in their shared work.

A father works with Jesus, particularly in his own child, side by side, offering all his work to Jesus so that by means of this self-giving love, he will assist his children in becoming temples of the Holy Spirit.

There will be times when we attempt to "craft the cross of self-giving love" and the crafting ends in conflict. Often, when we attempt to be a gift to our children by means of work, we will experience tension and may become impatient, particularly with their lack of experience. Indeed, the very experience that was intended to unite us with our children becomes the context for disagreements, frustrations, and arguments. There will be occasions when working side by side with our children actually drives a wedge between dad and child.

For example, I recently decided to add an extension pipe to my basement's sump pump exit line. During our rainy season the sump pump typically sends hundreds of gallons of water into my backyard, rendering it a virtual swamp. My daughter Zelie, my would-be snow shoveler who is now eight, asked if she could help. I agreed. The project appeared to be relatively simple: dig a drain-tile trench, add the extension pipe to the current exit drainpipe, and bury it in the ground.

Since the project was so easy, I decided to make it a bit more challenging by digging the trench while it was raining (no project is easy for me).

As I proceeded to do so, my shovel, my shoes, my hands, and my wheelbarrow became caked with mud—heavy mud. I was becoming frustrated with myself. *What idiot would decide to dig a drain-tile ditch while it's raining, and be stupid enough to have his child help?* Finally, after digging the trench, I attempted to fit the extension pipe on the existing drainpipe. There was, however, a little problem. The openings on both of the pipes appeared to be the same size—or at least so close in size that it seemed impossible to slide the extension pipe onto the existing drainpipe. It was during the second attempt to do so that Zelie said, "That isn't going to work." Again during the third failed attempt to slide one pipe over the other, she said with complete confidence, "That isn't going to work." It was only after the sixth time she said, "That isn't going to work" that in frustration I responded, "You are so much like your mother!"

Zelie was silent for a moment. I felt awful. She then broke the silence with a question. "Why am I like mom?" To which I answered, "Because . . . you're beautiful."

We will all fail. We will all make mistakes—but it is imperative that we persevere and try again. Sacred Tradition recounts that Jesus fell three times on His way to Calvary, and we can learn from this that we are likewise called to begin again, again, and again.

While it is true that our children will learn much from us as they work alongside of us, it is also true that we will learn much from them. Jesus, while serving Joseph, learned from Joseph, and Joseph, while serving Jesus, learned much from Jesus. In fact, it is our children who, while we serve them, will teach us some of the most valuable lessons there are to learn.

Years ago, Anna Marie arrived home after her school day. She is typically a very joy-filled, smiley, friendly girl. However, on this day, as she got off the bus, she was sobbing uncontrollably. We eventually discovered that one of her classmates was mocking her, telling her that she would never walk. Though Anna Marie had spent her young life in a wheelchair, she never considered the reality that she would never walk. Her classmate's words broke her little, innocent, naive heart. She could not be consoled. She cried from the time she was dropped off until dinner, and through dinner. Finally, I took her into her bedroom, sat on her bed, laid her body across my lap, and rocked her as she cried.

Then she opened her eyes and caught sight of the crucifix hanging on her bedroom wall. She stopped crying and gradually a smile crept across her face. Confused, I asked her, "Anna Marie, why are you smiling?" To which she responded, "I think I understand now . . . I get to suffer with Jesus . . . and that makes me happy."

Now I was the one who was crying. It was one of the most valuable lessons I have ever learned and it came from my victim soul, my handicapped, special-needs daughter. It was as though she was saying, "I know the secret to living a life of greatness! It is to suffer with God. God's glory is self-giving love! Won't you be my Simon and help me carry this cross? Won't you help me offer this suffering for souls?"

Within the context of serving our children we are afforded some of the greatest insights.

Resilience and perseverance are necessary characteristics of a father who desires to see his children become holy temples of the living God. We all fail, fall, and make mistakes, but the father who succeeds is the man who learns from his failures and, by God's grace, gets up and tries again.

The human father is the face of the Father that our children cannot see.

Blessing the Child to Build the Temple

We began this chapter by saying that we don't want our children to merely survive, but rather, we want them to thrive. Noah's curse upon Ham dramatically impacted his life and the life of his descendents. From that point on, Ham was simply trying to survive. This survival was expressed in the form of selfishness, and this selfish disposition was transmitted to his son, and from his son to his grandson.

We've also discovered that the key to actually living is to become a sincere gift. In fact, the key to having a life of joy, peace, and fulfillment is discovered by giving oneself away for the sake of others and for the sake of God. In other words, "You use, you lose. You give, you live."

Recall that there are several ways that we can do that, and become the face of the Father that they cannot see. One of the most important ways in which a father communicates the Father's love is by touching his children. So often, particularly in our American culture, men are somewhat apprehensive, if not fearful, of touching their children. If our children do not physically experience their father's love by means of hugs, kisses on the forehead, or pats on the back, they will attempt to obtain that physical touch in disordered ways.

I can recall as a young boy being with my father at functions that demanded reverent silence. Often, in the midst of the event, at a particular moment when it would be terribly rude to make a squeak, my dad would grab my knee with his signature deadlock grip. I wanted to scream! And yet, because of that grip, and the smirk on his face, I knew that he loved me.

One of the most important expressions of the father's touch is the fatherly blessing. It is one of the greatest powers in that it has the ability to assist his child in his efforts to become giving so that he may be living. The human father has been granted the authority to transmit grace, God's fatherly blessing. To be clear, God is the source of every blessing—not man. Yet each father should trust that he has a vital role as the transmitter of this blessing.

Often, fathers neglect to bless their children, or worse, do not believe that they have been divinely ordained with

the power to transmit God's blessing. From Abraham to
Isaac, Isaac to Jacob, Jacob to Joseph—down to St. Joseph
son of Jacob, who transmitted the divine blessing to Jesus
—God the Father has given the human father the power
to transmit His blessing to his children.

Recall that we fathers communicate the Father's love
by means of looking, listening, and touching, and that the
three basic contexts for looking, listening, and touching are
playing, working, and praying. When we bless our children, we communicate God the Father's love by touching
them within the context of praying. In other words, we become the touch of the Father that our children cannot feel.

Joseph's Blessing

According to Jewish tradition, on the eve preceding the
Sabbath, the father of a Jewish family summons his children
and invokes upon them, in the name of the Lord, a special
blessing.

Joseph, being a "just man," who fulfilled the law and
followed his ancestral customs, certainly participated in
such traditions by summoning Jesus to himself, placing his
hands on the head of his beloved Son, and invoking God's
blessing upon Him.

As Jesus allowed Himself to be baptized by John the
Baptist, so also Christ allowed Himself to be blessed by
Joseph to indicate that every child should be blessed by his
father and that every father should bless his child. By
blessing his child, the human father becomes a vital link
between his child and the heavenly Father.

Joseph's example is a fitting testimony to fathers who
sense their own unworthiness to confer the divine blessing
upon their children. Regardless of how great the child is,
or how unworthy the father is, the father is ordained by

God to bestow the fatherly blessing. If it was fitting for God the Son to be blessed by a human father, how much more is it fitting that we human fathers are to bless our children?

In this act of summoning our children to ourselves, placing our hands upon their heads, tracing the sign of the cross upon their forehead, and calling upon God to bless them, our children will feel the Father that they cannot touch, listen to the voice of the Father that they cannot hear, and know the Father whom they cannot see.

We don't need to complicate the matter by making the blessing an intricate, time-consuming, formulaic ritual. The act of blessing is quite simple and yet has profound effects. First, choose a time to bless your children—perhaps before bedtime, or before their school day. Regardless, it is important to schedule a time of day in which you bless your children, and be committed to granting the blessing every day.

Second, keep the prayer simple. The main elements for the invocation are: Bless them in the name of the Father, the Son, and the Holy Spirit. Ask God to bless them with His peace, mercy, and favor, that they may become temples of God's glory. Perhaps you can memorize a biblical blessing, such as: "The LORD bless you and keep you: The LORD make his face to shine upon you, and be gracious to you: The LORD lift up his countenance upon you, and give you peace" (Num. 6:24–26).

Third, be consistent and have faith that God the Father will bestow tremendous blessings upon your children through you, His transmitter of fatherly love.

Not Knowing the Results

There is a story of a high school football player whose father attended every one of his son's practices and every one of his son's games—despite being blind. Week in and week out, the father consistently came to "watch" his son start as a middle linebacker without ever actually seeing him play. Eventually, the son's team won the semifinals and were sent on to play in the state championship game. Shortly before the big game, the son's father died. Disheartened and crushed, the son remained resolute and determined to play in the championship game because he knew that by playing he would be honoring his father.

The game was a nail-biter, and with only a couple of minutes remaining in the fourth quarter, the son's team was down by a field goal. The opponent's quarterback dropped back in the pocket, looking to pass, but feeling pressure from the defensive line, threw a hurried pass down the middle of the field. The son, who happened to be in the right spot at the right time, intercepted the pass and ran forty yards for the game-winning touchdown.

As his teammates celebrated, lifting him on their shoulders, screaming and cheering and tossing him about, the son began to sob. His teammates asked him, "Why are you crying? You won the state championship! We won!" The son responded, "My dad, my dad—he went to every one of my practices and every one of my games, but could never see me play, but today, he sees me from heaven. My dad sees my glory from heaven."

In the end, when our days on earth come to completion, and those challenging yet rewarding days of fatherhood come to a close, we may, indeed, be blind to the full effect and impact that our fatherhood and our fatherly blessing has had upon our children. But one day, from the realm of the eternal Fatherland, we can hope to see with clear vision our children, victorious and glorious in fulfilling their mission of becoming temples of the eternal Father's glory.

NOTES

Secret 1: Rediscover Fatherhood

[1] Vmalpan.blogspot.com, *Jawbone of an Ass and St. John Maria Vianney*, www.vmalpan.blogspot.com/2009/08.

[2] Cf. Rebekah Levine Coley, et al., "Fathers' and Mothers' Parenting Predicting and Responding to Adolescent Sexual Risk Behaviors," *Child Development*, 80:3 (May/June 2009), 808–27.

[3] Baptist Press, statistics from Focus on the Family Publishing, *Promise Keepers at Work*, www.bpnews.net/15630.

[4] Researchers at Columbia University found that children living in two-parent household with a poor relationship with their father are 68% more likely to smoke, drink, or use drugs compared to all teens in two-parent households. Teens in single mother households are at a 30% higher risk than those in two-parent households. Source: "Survey Links Teen Drug Use, Relationship with Father." *Alcoholism & Drug Abuse Weekly* 6 September 1999: 5.

[5] thefatherlessgeneration.wordpress.com.

[6] St. Catherine of Siena, letter 368. As referenced by Pope John Paul II, World Youth Day address, August 2000, Rome.

[7] See *Joseph and Jesus. A Theological Study of Their Relationship*, Francis L. Füas S.J., *Franciscan Studies* 13, no. 2–3 (June–September).

Secret 2: Set the Pace of Self-Giving Love

[1] John Paul II, *Man and Woman He Created Them: A Theology of the Body* (Boston: Pauline Books & Media, 2006).

2 John Paul II, General Audience, November 14, 1979.

3 Father Boniface Hicks, O.S.B., *Blessed Be St. Joseph Her Most Chaste Spouse* (Downingtown, Pa.: Theology of the Body Institute, 2012).

4 John Paul II, *Man and Woman He Created Them*, 300.

5 St. Augustine, *On Christian Doctrine*, Book I.

Secret 3: Spiritually Adopt
Your Children

1 Charisma News, *Does Fatherlessness Produce Faithless Atheists*, Kimberly Winston, charismanews.com/42400.

2 Janet Smith, lecture, October 31, 2015, St. Pius X Church, Rock Island, Ill.

3 J. Bryant, D. Brown, "Use of Pornography," *Pornography: Research Advances and Policy Considerations* (Hillsdale, N.J.: Erlbaum, 1989), 25–55; cited in Citizen Link, *The New Normal? Youth Exposure to Online Pornography*, January 27, 2012, www.citizenlink.com/2012/01/27.

4 Dr. Taylor Marshall, *80% Catholic Youth Leave the Church (and how to fix it)*, www.taylormarshall.com.

5 John Paul II, *Redemptor Hominis*, 6.

6 Emery de Gaal, *The Theology of Pope Benedict XVI: The Christocentric Shift* (Basingstoke, United Kingdom: Palgrave Macmillan, 2010), 79.

Secret 4: Embrace the Silence

1 John Paul II, *Crossing the Threshold of Hope* (Toronto: Knopf, 1994), 228.

2 St. John of the Cross, *Spiritual Maxims* II, 21.

3 C. S. Lewis, *The Screwtape Letters* (San Francisco: Harper One, 2015), 120.

Secret 6: Sacrifice in Secret

[1] *Gaudium et Spes*, Pastoral Constitution on the Church in the Modern World, Second Vatican Council, 1965, 24.

Secret 7: Build and Bless

[1] John Paul II, *Gift and Mystery*, 20.
[2] *Gaudium et Spes*, 24.
[3] John Paul II, *Guardian of the Redeemer*, 22.

A VIRTUAL TOOL BOX FOR DADS

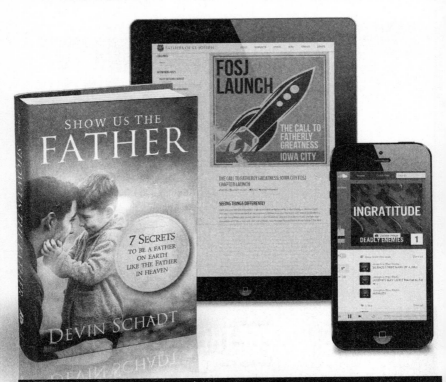